Outside the Tee Box
My Personal Journey and Secrets of Success in the Golf Business

Murray McCourt

OUTSIDE THE TEE BOX

My Personal Journey and Secrets of Success in the Golf Business

Copyright © 2023 by Murray McCourt

All rights reserved.

No part of this book may be reproduced, distributed, or transmitted in any form or by any means, including photocopying, recording, or other electronic or mechanical methods, without the written permission from the author, except in the case of brief quotations embodied in a book review.

Cover Design by Will Severns

Part and Chapter title page designs by Freepik

Streamline Books

www.WriteMyBooks.com

Paperback ISBN: 9-798-3866-3775-0

Hardcover ISBN:

March 23rd, 2023

I would like to dedicate this book to a few people... My wife Jessica and son Luke. The love and support that I get from my family is incredible. I cherish them both greatly.

My parents Dave and Evelyn, for their support and encouragement for me to chase my dreams.

The management team at The Ranch: Superintendent Derek Senkow, Head Professional Shaun Piercey, Office Manager Lynn Riley, Events/Clubhouse Manager Adam Wisser, and Kitchen Manager Howard Li. This team is phenomenal, and we have accomplished so much together. I appreciate all they do to help make The Ranch all that it is each and every day.

Kraig Kann for pushing me to move forward with writing a book. His support and encouragement was so helpful getting me out of my comfort zone to pursue writing this book.

Contents

Foreword — xi
Phil Berube, CEO of Alberta Golf and Former Executive Director of the PGA of Alberta

Part One
The Front Nine
My Personal Journey and Highlights

1. Murray's Big Drive — 3
2. Teeing Up the Ultimate Golf Career — 17
3. A Time of Transition — 30
4. Building Relationships at Nanton Golf Club — 42
5. Once a Bison, Always a Bison — 52
6. You are What You Eat — 61
7. Elevating the Food & Beverage Experience at Your Golf Club — 67
8. Life at The Ranch — 77
9. Sunday Matches — 85

Part Two
The Back Nine
Business Lessons Learned

10. The Layers of Your Brand — 95
11. Why Value is So Valuable — 111
12. Rubbing Shoulders, Shaking Hands — 123
13. The Power of Innovation — 131

14. Creating a Friendly, Inclusive
     Course Atmosphere   141
15. Empowering Your Employees   150
16. Taking a Swing at Corporate Sales   154
17. The Pandemic Impact on Business   158
18. Giving Back to the Industry   165

Afterword   177
About the Author   181

Foreword
Phil Berube, CEO of Alberta Golf and Former Executive Director of the PGA of Alberta

Meeting great people and remaining in touch with them throughout the journey is one of life's most rewarding gifts. This is especially true in the golf industry. When I made the decision to move to Calgary in 1998 I met one of those people, someone who was willing to give me a chance to succeed in this business – a business which at times can seem nearly impossible to find any work-life balance. That person was Dave Mayes, a transplanted Scot from Glasgow on the verge of retirement who was without a doubt one of the kindest people anyone in the golf industry has ever had the privilege to meet.

Dave had been hired by the PGA of Alberta in 1986 on a part time basis and became the first full time executive director in 1992. Armed with three banker boxes full of membership records for the two hundred or so professionals working throughout the province and a heart about the same size as those three boxes combined, Dave went to work and built a family – a family where every golf professional throughout the province was treated the same. Whether you were a long-time head pro working at a private club or a young assistant just getting started in the business, Dave went to bat for each and every member, every single day. Promoting them, supporting them, providing them with career advice and most of all just listening to them. And this is how the family of golf professionals grew to become one of the strongest golf associations to this day.

I had taken my own chances by leaving my first real world job following university and moving from Montreal to Calgary. But it was a risk I was willing to take and with no strings attached over the next three years I would work alongside Dave as he showed me the ropes while mapping out his retirement. I took over as Executive Director of the PGA of Alberta in 2002 and it was the people, so many of them, who helped me succeed in that role for the ensuing eleven years. Our small staff team punched above its weight. We attracted a number of strong committee and board members who kept the family together. We would meet regularly to continue building upon the foundation that Dave had left for us, making decisions to further the golf profession in the province on behalf of what had then grown to a membership of 550 pros.

One of those pros was Murray McCourt.

Not too far down the road from Calgary was the Nanton Golf Club, a small-town country golf course where Murray had once told me that selling hot dogs and making sure people were having fun on the golf course were larger priorities for him as Head Professional at the time. He didn't have a handful of Assistants to help him run the business. He couldn't escape from work for a day and compete in one of the thirty tournaments being run by the Association. He was working open to close for six and sometimes seven days a week just to make ends meet. "Who me, volunteer for a committee, are you kidding me right now?" Straight from the horse's mouth.

When I first met Murray he told me in a pretty straightforward manner what he thought about the politics in the golf industry and his views on employment opportunities for young golf pros. I wouldn't say Murray was critical of the Association at all—he was one of the most down to earth deep thinkers I had come across. With his ability to ask the right questions and get me to think about new perspectives, he opened my eyes up to other aspects of the golf business very quickly. From the moment I met him I knew he was an incredible resource the rest of the PGA Members needed to tap into, someone who possessed a passion for sharing his knowledge and a work ethic that, if replicated, would help others succeed.

    He just needed the vehicle. So I persevered and eventually Murray agreed to join our Board of Directors, overseeing our promotions portfolio. I assured him that most of the work would be during the off-season from November to March and would not jeopardize his job at Nanton. He either believed me or he didn't care – either way if he was going to do anything at all, he was committed, he was all in.

    His impact on the PGA of Alberta was immediate and it became obvious to everyone at the first promotions meeting to discuss the

Calgary golf show why Murray was so successful in his own right. As a people person oozing with confidence from a business perspective, he empowered everyone involved with the committee to achieve success – he had some of the youngest golf professionals volunteering their time for the greater good of the Association, taking on some of the most significant financial and public relations responsibilities, riding a wave of success in the mid 2000s that saw tens of thousands of people flood through the front doors of the show, looking for lessons, booking trips and getting great deals on golf equipment.

Back to his career at the golf course, his business success at Nanton led him to an opportunity up the highway in Edmonton where he was hired as the General Manager/Executive Professional, and a few years later became one of the owners at The Ranch, one of the province's top end public golf courses. He made the move but his willingness to remain connected to the PGA of Alberta didn't stop and in a whirlwind of activity over the next few years he quickly ascended to becoming chair of the Association's largest PR initiatives – overseeing both the Calgary and Edmonton golf shows.

Following one of these shows in March, we were celebrating together when I informed him of the difficult decision I had made to leave my role with the PGA of Alberta at the end of the season to explore an opportunity in the Toronto area. His reaction was pretty much what I expected it to be, "What, you're leaving us? But we're just getting started!"

That fall Murray organized one of the best evenings my wife and I have ever experienced at a local restaurant where we were able to enjoy a private dinner and personally thank the 150 golf professionals who showed up. Incredible people. As it turns out the move was a short-lived experiment as we quickly realized the impact the golf industry and the people in Alberta had on our growing family. We returned to Calgary two years later with our two sons and I've been really fortunate to be enjoying my current role as the CEO of Alberta Golf ever since. Connecting the pros with the amateurs, I think this could work.

One of my first phone calls when I came back to Alberta in 2016 was to Murray. He asked what I saw in the challenge and was intrigued at the prospect of being part of the dramatic changes being presented. At the time amateur

Foreword

bodies around the world were facing criticism from clubs over the value proposition being offered in an industry that was seeing fewer competitive players embrace the game. Times had changed and the clubs were now chasing the recreational market where golf was being sold as a fun experience, falling on the family's ledger as "entertainment" rather than buried under dad's "miscellaneous" expenses.

The Ranch had no members and no involvement at all with Alberta Golf and I knew that. Murray's business was running like a well-oiled machine, tournament rounds were sky high and the overall social golf experiences were adding to Murray's bottom line. He was building merchandising apps and selecting pairing wines, he wasn't all that interested in what the governing bodies had to say about where the red stakes needed to be on his property.

But Murray is a smart businessman and most importantly a great friend. In the spirit of camaraderie, innovation and calculated risk-taking he listened to the changes being proposed and gave me a chance. I assured him the amateur bodies around the world were looking to have a greater impact on the larger golf market and striving to become more relevant and responsive.

Fast forward a few years and The Ranch now has more than 150 Members of Golf Canada and has played host to a number of provincial championships during the past five years, including three marquee events – the Men's Amateur, the Women's Amateur and the Men's Mid Amateur Championships. The club continues to secure volunteers for the Association and generally everyone involved has helped Alberta Golf carve a path forward in better serving the recreational golf market.

Whether it's his Sunday morning radio show or the consulting advice Murray provides to his peer owner-operators one-on-one, there is always something forward-thinking coming out of his corner of the world to which we always pay particularly close attention.

A lot of people in the golf business have a general understanding about how long it takes to build a credible brand, through perseverance and hard work, eventually making a positive impact on the game. There are only a select few who actually do something about it, and Murray is definitely one of those people.

Foreword

His willingness and ability to share broadly what has worked for him is limited only by the channels available. For those who truly want to understand how to make it, this publication will be a keeper.

Part One
The Front Nine
My Personal Journey and Highlights

Murray's Big Drive

Every family has their "thing." Sometimes it's a shared hobby. Sometimes it's a genetic trait. Sometimes it's a laugh or the way everyone says the same phrase. My family is known for a particular characteristic: hard work.

I learned about hard work from my parents at an early age. My father, Dave McCourt, is a steam engineer by trade. He worked at the gas plant in a tiny town called Nevis, which was about a 20-minute drive from Stettler, my hometown in the province of Alberta, Canada. He eventually worked his way up to being in charge of the entire plant. He also had a part-time hobby business called Woodcraft By Dave. He had a workshop in our home where he made incredible souvenirs out of wood that were sold in several gift shops across Western Canada. During the week, my dad would go to his regular job, come home and have supper, and then spend the rest of his nights and weekends in the workshop, creating intricate woodworking mementos. Now that he's retired, my dad has a bigger building in Stettler where he works and restores old vehicles.

My mother, Evelyn McCourt, is a piano teacher. She had a large number of students each year when I was growing up. She would often have students come over for lessons before school started, on their lunch break, right after school, and into the evenings. Sometimes, she taught lessons on weekends, too. Mom's piano lessons took place in our home, and I remember that I would often get woken up when her students started to play.

Both of my parents were always busy working—and they worked hard. But they were also doing the things they loved and were passionate about. Growing up in this environment certainly had an impact on my future.

From the time I was young, I always had something in my life that I was extremely passionate about. I cultivated the skill of working hard thanks to the great example set by my parents. Over the years, most of my passions have involved sports in some way. Growing up in Stettler, Canada, a town of 4,500-5,000 residents known as "The Heart of Alberta," there were tons of activities and sports, especially outdoors.

Funny enough, I actually got my parents into sports—not the other way around. I am a self-proclaimed sports nut. I wanted to play sports all the time and also watched my favorite teams on TV. As a child, I played many sports, including baseball, bowling, football, and hockey. My parents were always supportive and came to watch as many of my games as they could. If they weren't working, they would watch sports on the television with me, too. In fact, they became lifelong fans of the Edmonton Oilers NHL team and the Edmonton Elks CFL team (formerly the Edmonton Eskimos) by watching them on TV with me.

Each Sunday, "America's Team," the Dallas Cowboys, played on TV in our part of Canada, which led me to become a diehard fan from a very young age. On Sundays, my family always went to church together. When I was very young, I told my parents that I could no longer go to church on Sundays because the football games were on TV, and I didn't want to miss anything. At this point, I was a huge Dallas Cowboys fan. My father thought this was fine, and he stayed home with me. It was perfect—I never missed a single play of my beloved Dallas Cowboys or Edmonton Eskimos football games, even at six years old.

As a kid, my other favorite team was the Chicago Blackhawks, but it didn't start out that way. At the time, there were only 18 teams in the National Hockey League, and none of them were located in Alberta where I grew up. I was initially a Montreal Canadiens fan, and Guy Lafleur was my favorite player. But once dynamic superstar hockey player Denis Savard was drafted to the Chicago Blackhawks, I had to switch teams. I loved the way Savard played the game, and since he played for the Blackhawks, it made the change fairly easy. They've been my favorite hockey team ever since.

When I was in junior high school, a teacher wrote a comment on my report card once: "It's great to see the Blackhawks are climbing in the standings as Murray's marks are climbing as well." My passion for hockey was so strong that my school marks were impacted by the team's performance. To this day, I am still a diehard Chicago Blackhawks fan.

My best friend growing up was Terry Abel. He lived just down the street from my family, and we hung out all of the time as we grew up. One day when I was 13 years old, Terry suggested we go golfing. Stettler had a nine-hole golf course that was a short bike ride across the highway from where we lived. I agreed to go with him, and we hopped on our bikes to go play. The first nine holes I ever played, I shot 71. Not too long after, we went to play again. I shot 73. We went a third time, and I skipped the 60s altogether and shot a 59. I was hooked, and golf quickly became a huge new passion of mine.

My early passion for golf developed mostly because I was able to get good at it really quickly. This made it fun to play! It also gave me something to do with my best friend Terry, and it kept us busy during the summers. Who knew at this time that this passion would last a lifetime and eventually become my career? I certainly didn't.

As time passed, my passion for golf was brought on by the enjoyment of playing various courses. I truly enjoyed playing courses for the first time. I also love the social aspects of golf, where you can genuinely spend four hours with family, friends, peers, business contacts, and others with little distraction outside of playing the game.

In business today, my passion for golf is striving to improve and get better—both personally in my own knowledge and growth, and professionally in the business of the golf course. Nowadays, I love the challenge of fixing and solving issues on the business side. Whether it's finding ways to become more efficient on expenses or developing creative ways to grow the business, I enjoy every opportunity to improve. I'm also extremely passionate about creating a positive culture in the work environment that encourages personal growth for our team, and working together to ensure that the pillars of our business translate to a great experience for our guests. There will be more on that later in the book.

One day, my parents took me to a local store in Stettler to buy me a set of golf clubs, since golf was becoming something I always wanted to do.

They were nothing special, but they were fine for the time being.

Terry and I started golfing a lot. Every day, we would ride our bikes to the course and walk for nine holes. Some days we played a full 18. On really good days, we played 36 holes; some days we even played 54 holes. Terry and I were hooked—we loved it. Playing as much as we did, I improved very quickly. The scores were dropping, and I started shooting in the 40s by the end of that first summer.

We picked up right where we left off the following year. We also changed the way we gripped the clubs during a swing. We had both been playing with a 10-finger grip and had read that we needed to be using an "overlap" or "interlock" grip if we really wanted to get better. One day, Terry and I decided we would try it and stick with it no matter how bad we played. It took some time, but we practiced with the new grip and continued to improve.

Eventually, I told my parents that I really loved golf and needed to get some decent golf clubs. The beginner clubs weren't doing the trick anymore. What I wanted was a big investment for a teen just getting into golf, so they took me to the bank and helped me get a loan to get the clubs I wanted to buy.

We headed over to Par T Golf in Red Deer, a bigger town about a 45-minute drive away from small-town Stettler. I got some Ping Eye 2 irons, which at the time were known as some of the best irons on the market. I also got some completely custom-fit woods with titanium shafts. Although custom woods are considered the norm now, it was a brand-new concept for golfers back then.

I had the best of the best at the time, and I was excited to see how well I could play with my new sticks. At this stage of my life, I could hit the ball up over 300 yards. I wish I could still do that today. I could tell that the new clubs were worth the investment, and they certainly helped my game in a big way, compared to what I was using previously.

I eventually wanted to see if I could make a career out of my passion, as my parents did. With some research, I made my plan to become a golf professional.

When I was in ninth grade, we were asked to fill out a form for the yearbook that included sharing what we wanted to do for a career when we were older. I remember thinking long and hard about writing down the truth: I wanted to be a golf professional. However, I decided to write, "parole officer" instead because I thought everyone would make fun of me if I wrote "golf professional" in the yearbook.

I knew that was what I wanted to do, though. I tailored all my high school classes so that they would set me up in the best way possible to achieve my dream of being a golf professional. I filled up my schedule with classes like Accounting, Business Law, and Typing. I got crazy good at typing in school, despite my 10th-grade teacher trying to convince me to drop the class. I had broken my hand playing hockey and he did not want me to learn to type with one hand, so he wanted me to drop the class. I refused to drop it and stayed out of the class until my hand was healed. I caught up quickly and ended up going to the high school provincial championships in typing. To this day, I still type extremely quickly and accurately, and I certainly use that skill every day.

In high school, I chose to do the minimum number required of core classes so I had the opportunity to take as many classes that would help me as a golf professional. I really hated science and only five credits of science were required to get a high school diploma. I took Biology 10, and I ended up getting a grade of 50 percent, which was just enough to get my five credits. My teacher was a golf buddy, and I am sure that was the only reason I got a passing grade as science was never my thing.

In ninth grade, I started working as a cook at the local Dairy Queen. I held this position my entire high school career. We had so many amazing people that worked together at DQ for many years, and we had so much fun together both at work and away from work. Great friendships developed. Working in that environment enabled me to learn about everything it takes to run a business smoothly.

The biggest things I learned while working at DQ were the importance of working together as a team and the positive culture that good teamwork creates. Having a great team is a key part, but ensuring the team has the structure and detail of all that needs to happen during a shift is super important to be successful. The little things—like ensuring everything is stocked—are imperative. Running out of things in the middle of a rush can throw off your entire rhythm and ultimately give the guests a negative experience if their food comes out slowly.

Don Rumberger owned the DQ. He was a big golfer, and we became golf buddies over the years. He was such a great boss. Perhaps, for me, it was because we had golf and sports in common. But he also took an interest in me as a person. He knew about my passion for golf and would schedule my work shifts around my golf tournament schedule. It was a lot, but he was fine accommodating that request. Because of this kindness, I worked hard for him to ensure I did all I could to do right by him in return. I felt that was an extremely valuable lesson for me, as I've always tried my best to get to know the people I've worked with and treat them well so that they know how much they are appreciated.

My routine was pretty much set through my high school years: school, golf, and working at the Dairy Queen. Sure there was hanging out with my friends and partying as well, but my main focus was golf. I loved it so much and will always have my pal Terry to thank for introducing me to this amazing game. I'd play golf after school in the evenings and on weekends until summer hit. In the summers, I'd play all day, every day. I worked at Dairy Queen a lot more in the winter, as my golf schedule eased up.

My golf game continued to improve. When I was 15, I was mostly shooting in the 30s for nine holes and sometimes I'd shoot par. Once in a while, I'd even shoot under par. At 15, I started playing in golf tournaments. I played in pretty much every Junior Open within a reasonable driving distance to Stettler. The vast majority of tournaments took place in the summer, which was good because it didn't interfere with school at all. I played in the Alberta Junior Championship, the Saskatchewan Junior Championship, the Central Alberta Amateur Championship, and the Alberta Amateur Championship. I also played in events at the Stettler Elks Golf & Country Club. If I had to guess, I played between 20 and 30 tournaments per year. Most of them took place in the summer. I won a few tournaments here and there.

I started looking to play in Men's Amateur events even though I was a junior in high school. I also started playing in the Men's League at the golf course in Stettler. This wasn't well received by all of the adults. But I appreciated the opportunity to play with adults and gained valuable knowledge and experience. It gave me more opportunities to play in a more competitive environment and with a variety of people. Stettler also lacked a driving range, so I had no range to practice on—this just gave me the excuse to play that many more rounds of the game. I became golf buddies with many of the members of the Men's League and continued to play as much as possible.

I do recall that I placed second in tournaments way too many times (in my opinion). I often wondered if I just didn't know how to win. For example, I always wanted to win the Stettler Mens Open, even though I mostly played it as a junior. Although I never won, I placed second several times.

A job that my dad had always given me at home was to cut the grass. Every day, I was getting up and riding my bike to the golf course. I was playing golf, practicing all day, and riding my bike back home in the dark. My dad would always get mad at me for not cutting the grass, but I kept avoiding it because I just wanted to play golf. He would eventually cut the grass himself when it got too long. He was always mad at me for skipping out on my household chores, but I knew deep down he was not that mad. He was happy that I was following my passion. He and my mom were both extremely supportive of what I wanted to do. They encouraged me to play the game and supported me in my education and career choices.

High school finished well for me. I was focused on taking classes that I envisioned would benefit me in my future in the golf business. My grades were high as I was engaged and focused on the classes that I thought would benefit me moving forward. I continued to play golf during the summers, hockey during the winters, and I also worked at the Dairy Queen until I graduated. I was optimistic, as my vision for the future in the golf world was becoming more clear.

Teeing Up the Ultimate Golf Career

After graduating high school, there was no secondary schooling available for golf in Canada. If you wanted to be a golf professional, you just got a job at a course and worked for a pro who was part of the Canadian Professional Golf Association (now called PGA of Canada). Then, you'd do an apprenticeship program that was administered by the CPGA that had educational components, in addition to a myriad of other requirements. There was also a certain amount of hours you were required to work for a head pro before you completed the apprenticeship.

I saw an advertisement for the San Diego Golf Academy (SDGA) in *Golf Digest* magazine and started communicating with them when I was in Grade 9, or perhaps early Grade 10. I had read and learned that it was the most prestigious golf management school in the world. By going to SDGA, I knew it would set me apart from other people. Plus it would cut down some of the pieces to the apprenticeship program once I came home and started working in the industry. As part of my journey to becoming a golf professional, I knew that this was the place I wanted to go. This was exactly what I had planned since Grade 9.

I learned what I needed to do to help me get accepted to the school and tailored my high school classes around that. Because going to SDGA was my goal and top choice, I knew I was going to do everything that I could to ensure I got in. If that didn't work out, I likely would have tried to find a job at a course and go through the normal apprenticeship program. But I knew I wanted to do something to set myself apart from others and ensure that I would be successful in my career. In my mind, doing things the "regular" way wasn't really an option. After reaching 12th grade, it was time to put in my application to go to San Diego. I also applied to a school in Florida called the Golf Academy of the South.

One morning, I was in Al Lagore's law class and there was a knock on the door. Al was a golf buddy, and after answering the door, he took the opportunity to embarrass me by announcing to the class, "Murray, your mother is at the door." Ugh. I was both confused at why she would be there and mortified that it was advertised to the entire classroom. When I got to the door, I saw a big envelope in her hand and recognized the San Diego Golf Academy logo on the front. She said that she thought I would not want to wait to see this. I grabbed the envelope out of her hand. It was a very thick envelope with a lot of paper. I read the first word, "Congratulations!" I knew at that moment that my goal and dream of the past several years had come true. I was moving to San Diego, California, to go to the school I wanted to attend with everything in me (I was also accepted to the Golf Academy of the South, but declined the offer). San Diego was so well-known and was "the" place to go for golf education.

Immediately, I threw the entire package of papers in the air, making a huge mess for my mom to clean up while I started running through the school screaming and jumping in the air. Teachers were coming out of their classrooms to see what the big commotion was about. When they saw how happy I was, they just left me to my personal celebration. Word traveled fast around the school. I was leaving Stettler behind and heading to San Diego.

In the end, living in the San Diego area and going to the SDGA was all I thought it would be, and much more. However, the transition was quite difficult. Moving from Stettler, Alberta, a small Canadian town of around 5,000 people, to a huge city like San Diego was a massive transition. There was no such thing as text messaging, emailing, FaceTime, or other modern ways of communicating. With that, I wrote a ton of letters, keeping in touch with friends back home. It was always a highlight to get the mail every day and receive letters from friends. I was homesick. But I was also meeting many great people, playing golf in the middle of winter, living a short drive to the beach, and getting a great education. I missed home, but I had the time of my life.

When I attended the SDGA, it was located on a 27-hole golf course which, at the time, was called Whispering Pines Golf & Country Club. Classes were a mix of business classes taught by professors, mostly from San Diego State University, and golf-specific classes. The instructors of the golf classes were mostly golf professionals. This part was so incredible. We were learning how to teach golf from instructors who taught players who played on the PGA and LPGA Tours. What an incredible opportunity!

There was no driving range at Whispering Pines. However, there was a massive range nearby where we could go practice, take lessons from some of the incredible instructors, and of course, learn how to teach the game. School would typically end around noon. I would grab a hot dog and a bottle of water for lunch at the snack shack prior to playing golf most afternoons. Every Friday was a tournament for those in the school. These tournaments were run by one of the classes where we were taught how to run golf tournaments. It's a rather effective way to learn how to run a golf tournament by doing it every Friday for a semester! We also had access to play other courses in the area. This was included in our tuition, so we got some variety in where we played. I also caddied some weekends at a nearby private golf course called Fairbanks Mountain Ranch. Caddying gave me the opportunity to play the course on Mondays.

Weekends were spent practicing golf, going to the beach, and heading down to Tijuana most Friday and Saturday nights. It was such a fun place to go and party. I did not drink alcohol at all while I lived in California, but I sure loved to dance! I was happy to be the designated driver every weekend to head down the highway to TJ and dance the nights away.

The two years at the SDGA flew by. To this day, I have some regrets about not taking full advantage of the opportunities I had living in California, but I feel we all make those mistakes by taking for granted the incredible things there are to see and do in our own backyards. However, I did spend a ton of time at the beach, as I lived very close to it. And I made it to Disneyland 16 times in two years. Everyone that visited me wanted to go there ... so we went.

I also played a bit of golf on the Golden State Tour while at SDGA. This experience quickly taught me that I was an exceptionally good player, but my career path was to be the golf professional that I always planned to be and not a touring pro. I grew up in a big hurry living on my own and being so far away from home. My game improved by leaps and bounds playing year-round, and I got a great education preparing me for my future in the golf business.

During my final semester at school, I started applying for positions as an Apprentice Professional. In the beginning, I had no idea how easy or difficult it would be to land a position. I sent my resume to many courses in Western Canada in hopes of landing in a great spot to use my education and get started in the career that I always wanted. It quickly became obvious that graduating from the San Diego Golf Academy with a degree in Golf Complex Operations and Management with Players Credentials made landing a position easy—I received 11 job offers.

I ended up choosing to accept a position at Wolf Creek Golf Resort because it was such a highly regarded golf course. Being ranked #14 in the entire country at the time was a huge draw for me. The golf course was amazing, and the opportunity to play it often was another huge perk. The course was in Ponoka, Alberta, only a 45-minute drive from Stettler. Its location so close to my hometown was a bonus. My sister, Heather, also lived in Ponoka so I knew that would help make the move there easier. Accepting the Wolf Creek position also gave me the opportunity to work with Clint Duff who is from Ponoka and was a classmate of mine in San Diego. We were great friends, and I thought it would be fun to work with him. It was an easy decision for me to choose to go to Wolf Creek to start my career as a golf professional.

After graduation from SDGA, I was so excited to get started as an assistant professional at Wolf Creek Golf Resort. I never realized how much I would miss not having winters and getting to play golf year-round, but that was not what was on my mind at the moment. I was set to earn $1,200 per month working at the number 14th ranked golf course in Canada ... How could life be any better?

I am so grateful for my time at Wolf Creek. The Vold family was amazing to work for and work with. One of my biggest takeaways from working with Ryan Vold and the rest of the family was hard work. It was a family-run business, and they were all there—a lot! I didn't know much about what Ryan was doing in his office all day, but I knew he was putting in so much time every day to make the business the best it could be. Kathy Vold was busy booking all of the golf tournaments and organizing them, and Lori Vold was looking after all of the cash outs and finances. Del Vold was often working with Lori on the finances, and she and Ralph Vold were there having lunch together almost every day. The Vold family put so much sweat and tears into the operation of Wolf Creek to make it all that it was. You don't become as highly regarded as Wolf Creek was without putting in a ton of time and effort. This was clear to see and helped me immensely in my journey.

Ryan had also hired Mike Lyons from the United States to come up to Ponoka and be a leader in the organization at Wolf Creek. Mike had been in the business for a long time. He was both an outstanding player and a great teacher of the game. Mike became a tremendous mentor for me. The long talks about golf and life were always memorable as we received box after box of inventory in the spring and every other opportunity I could get to spend time with him, soaking up his knowledge like a sponge. It was incredible listening to Mike share stories of his time on the Canadian Tour and his many memories of the legendary Moe Norman and their on-course battles.

With Mike at Wolf Creek, there was not

much opportunity for me to earn lesson revenue as he was widely sought after for his instruction. I did cherish the opportunity to do some traveling with Mike to teach clinics in some smaller communities around Central Alberta. I would also drive 40 minutes once per week to teach lessons in my hometown of Stettler. Both were great opportunities to get my feet wet in teaching lessons as a golf professional. Earning a few extra dollars was also hugely beneficial, as it was quite hard to make ends meet on just the wage of an assistant professional back then just as it is now.

The Alberta Open on the Canadian Tour was held at Wolf Creek during my three seasons there. It was another incredible opportunity for me to be around and involved in an event that brought many future stars on the PGA Tour to "The Wolf," as it was nicknamed. There was no question that plenty of Ryan Vold's time in his office was putting this event together. I appreciated every second of those weeks.

One very special memory I have of those events was Moe Norman coming by for a few days each year. Moe is known as perhaps the best Canadian golfer ever and one of the best ball strikers that ever lived. He was also autistic and quirky. Being able to spend time around such a legend was incredible. When he went to the driving range to hit balls, all of the Tour Players would stop what they were doing to watch Moe and appreciate how good he was. That's how much respect Moe had from Golf Professionals—everyone stopped as Moe explained his thoughts on the golf swing as he was hitting balls and practicing.

Another great memory from The Wolf was the opportunity to play the Rod Whitman-designed golf course as much as I did. It was such a treat. The Old Course was the first course that Rod Whitman ever designed, and he's one of the best golf course designers in the world. It has a fabulous layout with several spectacular holes that make it so fun to play! The "Old Course" will always have a special place in my heart. It's special to me because it's where I got my start as a golf professional.

It's hard not to appreciate the great design that it is. I likely didn't really know or understand what a busy golf course was at the time, as it always seemed busy at The Wolf. But by mid-afternoon, there was mostly an empty tee sheet that made it easy to play often. I certainly took advantage and played it hundreds of times. It is so easy to see how and why Rod Whitman has gone on to huge success as a course designer.

During my third season at The Wolf, a third 9-hole course opened that was known at the time as the "South 9." That was somewhat of a difficult year in the pro shop. When I told people the rotation they were playing included the new South 9, it was very rare that the players were not upset. Everyone wanted to play the original Wolf course. It was hard to not be understanding of their complaints as I didn't enjoy the South 9 either, but it was now part of the program at The Wolf, so for me it was what it was. I can't help but wonder if the course had stayed with the original, iconic 18 holes if that would have been a better choice with more positive outcomes.

After my third season at The Wolf, I made the decision that I was ready for a new experience with new challenges. The Vold family was great to me, and I loved playing the Old Course, and it helped set me up for my career. But my goal was to become a head professional as soon as possible. Although I was very young, I had high hopes for my future and felt that learning at a new facility would help me get there.

My parents still live in Stettler, but much of my family was in Edmonton, and that's where I decided I wanted to go. My grandparents, aunts, uncles, cousins, and extended family all lived in Edmonton. As job postings came out, I applied and very quickly two offers came my way. Windermere Golf & Country Club was a highly regarded private course in South Edmonton. Fort In View Golf Club was in Fort Saskatchewan. Both facilities offered me positions.

I will never know what other offers may have come my way, but I wanted to make a decision quickly to ensure I had a position in Edmonton. My decision to go to Fort In View shocked many. They were expanding to 27 holes, which was unusual. In fact, it's still pretty uncommon today—less than ten courses in Alberta have 27 holes. At that time, between Wolf Creek and the SDGA, I likely had the most 27-hole experience in the province, and they needed help figuring out how to best operate everything. With my knowledge and experience, I was able to command a much higher salary, and it was my understanding that I would have unlimited ability to earn money teaching there. With that, I was off to my next journey.

A Time of Transition

My time at Wolf Creek Golf Resort set me up for success. When I started at Fort In View, it was fun and rewarding to help get the course set up to operate as a 27-hole golf course. The staff was ready to learn how to maximize the revenue potential with extra holes and I was excited to teach them. I certainly felt like I was able to bring great value to the club with my experience, which helped set them up on the proper path to success.

I was very fortunate to meet and work with some great people while working at Fort In View. Walter Buck, a retired politician, was the owner of the golf course and he truly was a great man. He was a treat to be around and I had a great deal of respect for him. While there, I also had the privilege of working with several other golf professionals who went on to have successful careers in the industry including Art New, David Robinson, and Danny Grant.

The information that I had heard about there being an almost unlimited amount of teaching opportunities at Fort In View was accurate. On days when I opened the pro shop, I would have lessons booked every half hour from 2 p.m. until it was dark outside. If I worked the close shift, I would book lessons every half hour for two to four hours before I was scheduled to start my shift. This was extremely beneficial. For the first time in my young career, I was generating enough income to sustain a decent lifestyle and put a few dollars away to help get through the winter months.

Golf can be a tough business when you are first starting out as it is a seasonal business and the compensation is not always the greatest. To get beyond this stage, you need to show your value to the club. Everyone wants to get a bigger piece of the pie; but instead of just expecting to earn more money, how can you make the pie bigger? If you can be part of growing the business and the club is more profitable, then there will be an opportunity for you to work longer term with a higher salary. What can you offer that makes you more valuable? What if you could create a lesson or coaching program at your club through the winter that could bring additional revenue to the club and make financial sense to pay your salary year-round? What does your club do for corporate sales? Perhaps you could spend the offseason reaching out to your contacts and approaching local businesses to try to earn their branded product business. Profits from doing this successfully would help the club's bottom line and they would be more than happy to employ you over the winter. There is opportunity at all courses to earn year-round employment. You need to take responsibility for your own career by taking advantage of opportunities and showing your value. Don't just meet the bare minimum expectations in your role; elevate yourself and go above and beyond.

As a business, whether it is golf or not, it's important to stand out to your customers and differentiate yourself from the competition. A great term that I learned from my friend Kraig Kann is that you need to "elevate." Elevate what you do to a higher level to truly differentiate yourself from the competition. Doing this will help golfers choose to support and play at your course more than other courses if their experience is viewed as something better than the competition.

What are some ways that this can be done? If you do what everyone else does, why would someone choose to play your course over any of the other courses that compete with you for business? I'm jumping ahead a little bit, but in my current role at The Ranch Golf & Country Club, there are a few things we have done over the years that we consider to elevate the guest experience:

- The Ranch was the first course in the Edmonton area to have GPS on our power cart fleet. This is something that is much more commonplace today; however, it was a big deal when it first was available. The Ranch was the first to jump on board, and I believe it is still viewed by golfers as an elevation although it's not as unique as it once was.

- Having paved cart paths over the entire golf course. This is an elevation in many ways. Especially during wet conditions, The Ranch still allows golfers to use power carts and stay on the paths rather than force golfers to walk. Truly an elevated experience over what much of the competition can provide in that scenario.
- The Ranch Loyalty App is another great example. This app allows The Ranch to give golfers points for every dollar spent at The Ranch. These points can then be redeemed for valuable rewards, such as free golf, merchandise, food, and beverage at the club, and more. This is unique to The Ranch and absolutely makes a golfer's decision to choose The Ranch easier knowing that they get rewarded for their loyalty.

At The Ranch, we are always seeking to elevate even further. Many subtle things have and will continue to happen. The big focus is on offering rewards for our customer loyalty through our loyalty app and elevating their experience by offering unparalleled service. We want our team, no matter what department they are in, to go above and beyond to care for each guest to let them know they are very welcome here and that we appreciate their support. We also want to ramp up the knowledge with our loyalty program to ensure that all our guests know about the program and are offered points with every purchase they make.

We are focused on elevating our guests' experience at The Ranch, through rewarding loyalty and by offering unparalleled service. To reach those goals, it is imperative that our staff buy-in and do what is asked and expected of them when dealing with our guests. If we can achieve our goals, the staff are an integral part of that and with the elevation of the business, the staff will also elevate themselves in the industry by being part of the success. If the staff does not buy into what we are trying to accomplish, the opportunity for both the club and the staff has been lost and the opportunity to grow and learn from the experience is gone as well.

It is important to buy into what your club is

doing. Be a champion of the efforts and do your part to help the club succeed. The club's success also reflects on the staff. We have also given our staff different departments within the pro shop to take on as their own. They are to merchandise and promote their areas as they see fit to elevate the sales of these departments. This is a huge opportunity for our team to take a leadership role and help elevate our pro shop to a higher level. This is also a huge opportunity for them to show what they are capable of, how much they care, and ultimately how important they are to our operation and even the direction their future in the industry can go. Go-getters that would take an opportunity like this and run with it to ensure growth in their department would elevate themselves both within the club and outside the club as well. When given the opportunity to have responsibility, it is so important to make the most of it for the club's benefit as well as your own. Not taking these opportunities seriously and putting in your best effort to succeed would suggest that you are not prepared for leadership and growth in the industry. *If you do what everyone else does, then nothing sets you apart from anyone else and stifles your ability to grow in your industry. Set yourself apart!*

To attract customers, Fort In View used the "2 for 1" green fee strategy as their main marketing technique. For example, if the green fee was $50 for 18 holes, most of the time two golfers would play for $50. The club also spent a lot of money on advertising, which was smart. I took a look at this marketing strategy and would create my own plan just for fun—it was good practice for when I would eventually run Nanton and The Ranch (more on that later). Strategic marketing is something I've always been interested in, and it has become one of my strengths.

I was at a very interesting point in my career. I was just 23 years old, and after two seasons at Fort In View, I had five years of experience in the industry and earned my Class A Professional status. I had passed the Class A exam and completed the education and playability components that were required. After all that I had seen and learned, I felt that I was ready to be a head professional. At my age, perhaps I was thinking naively, but I made the decision that I was moving on from Fort In View and was going to land a head professional job.

My options were to find another club to work as an associate professional (you have your Class A status but aren't a head pro) or see if I could get a head pro job. Based on my education and experience, I felt that I was capable. I wasn't ready for a high-end course, but I figured I was ready for the head pro role at a smaller club. If I successfully earned a position, I could learn more on the job until I felt capable of running a bigger club. But I'd cross that bridge when I got there.

It's not like getting a job as a head professional was easy—jobs were hard to come by. Many head professionals stay at their club for a long time, especially if the club believes they do a good job and the golf professional is happy. A little movement does occur annually.

However, there was a transition going on in the industry where golf clubs started taking over the pro shop so that the club could profit off the operations instead of the golf professional. This was totally different from the previous norm, where the golf professional had the pro shop as their own private business. These types of situations were opening up a few jobs.

No matter what your goal may be in the golf business, whether it is to be a head professional, an executive professional, a teaching professional, or some other title in the business, there will always be huge competition for sought-after positions. To get your career going in the right direction, you want to view yourself as your own brand, just as the golf course does. You need to come up with ways to elevate yourself and become known in the industry. You need to stand out and separate yourself from your peers in the same way the golf courses need to separate themselves from the competition. If you do what everyone else does, then what makes hiring you a better choice than anyone else? How are you going to benefit the organization more than another candidate could? You do not want to be just another person, or you will never get to where you want to go in your career.

There are many ways that you can do this. Be active within your club and within the association. Get involved as much as you can. Play in events, attend education seminars, and volunteer where you can. Being involved will get you noticed. You also need to be involved at your club. Help take merchandising to a new level.

The junior program, the lost and found, marshaling—every area of your club could likely always be improved in some way. Be creative and think outside the box. Bring ideas forward that you think could bring improvement to your operation. Who knows, maybe your next idea will be a home run for the club.

I was the general manager of an extremely successful junior hockey team for 11 years. A saying that we used with our team consistently over the years was, "You get what you give." This saying is certainly something that fits well with a sports team, personal relationships, jobs, careers, and many other aspects of our lives. The more work and effort that you put into something, the more rewards you will get from your hard work. It is a very simple statement but holds true. If you want to be successful, put in the work. Success does not come easy as it needs to be earned. It is that much more exciting when your time and effort get rewarded by climbing the ladder in your industry. So elevate yourself, elevate your club. Put in the time and effort. Success in the golf industry will not be far behind.

I felt early on in the process that my hopes of landing a head pro job would come to fruition, as

I had the opportunity to meet and interview with a few clubs. Golf courses looking to hire a professional can post the job with the PGA of Canada and the provincial PGA—in this case, the PGA of Alberta. When I saw a job posting that interested me, I applied. New courses were opening, so I was in talks with an almost-ready-to-open course about their head pro opportunity. I also approached a few clubs in smaller areas that did not have a head pro.

Ultimately, I had my heart set on a job that would see me move away from Edmonton and my family's home base. The Nanton Golf Club just south of Calgary had offered me their head pro job. I was thrilled and excited about the opportunity. Everything that I had wanted and worked towards since Grade 9 was now my reality. At 23 years old, I was a head professional and could not wait to get started!

Building Relationships at Nanton Golf Club

At just 23 years old, I landed a job as a head professional, which is extremely rare. It's more common for golf professionals to land their first role as a head professional in their late 20s or early 30s. Accepting the head professional job at the Nanton Golf Club, a 45-minute drive south of Calgary, helped me see a lifelong dream come true. It ended up being a fabulous decision for my career, too. I'll always be grateful for the opportunity to work there and for the amazing people both at the golf course and in the community. While at Nanton, I gave the club my all—heart and soul—for 12 years to make it as successful as I could.

I got started at Nanton in the middle of

winter, with little knowledge of the facility or the needs and requirements of the pro shop, not to mention the members and guests. I felt excited and nervous. I wasn't sure what guest expectations would look like or what level of service they had previously experienced. I wanted to exceed member expectations, but without a clear starting point, it was difficult. However, I knew that surrounding myself with great people was a key to success in business. You can't run a successful operation on your own. You need great people to buy into your vision and passion for the business, which helps create a positive culture.

In the beginning, when I was stocking the pro shop at Nanton, I relied heavily on the sales reps that took the time to build a relationship with me when I was an assistant professional. Amazing reps like Kim Carrington and Steve Dyer were at the forefront of this for me, and those early relationships built lifelong customers for them.

Dave Mitchell, a local from Nanton, was another perfect person for me to work with as I got my feet wet. Dave was my right-hand guy in the pro shop. He knew everyone and he was well-liked and respected in the community. His familiarity with the course and the people helped make my transition much easier. Dave would have been an incredible golf professional and addition to the industry, but he never passed the playability requirements to join the PGA, which was the industry's loss. Dave eventually moved on to other things and I am sure he's been very successful in everything he has done.

Aaron Huppe and Clayton Gillespie were two others that I worked with after Dave. They were great ambassadors for the game and for the Nanton Golf Club. I also worked with Val Robinson, who at the time of this writing (17 years later!) still works at the Nanton Golf Club. I also worked with J.D. Scheller, who has gone on to have a successful career in the golf business. I appreciate everyone mentioned above and numerous others that helped me make the Nanton Golf Club all that we did.

The Nanton Golf Club and its members were a very social group. It was a fun place to be a part of. The members loved their golf—especially scrambles—and their time spent enjoying beverages on the course and at the 19th hole. My golf game suffered while at Nanton because there was always so much work to do. I played 18 holes every Tuesday, which was the men's league, and nine holes on Friday nights in the mixed league. I played PGA events and some member events, too, but there wasn't much time to practice or get out to play to keep my game where I liked it. As the sun went down, people gathered in the clubhouse. They were happy to have me join them for cocktails and conversation. It was a fun, relaxed atmosphere that was easy to enjoy.

A great example of the fun we had while working at Nanton was the epic water fight one Wednesday on ladies night. Earlier that day, Doug McDonald, the club president at the time, came to my office to visit. It was so hot outside that it was barely tolerable for many people to play golf. He had an idea to ambush the ladies with water guns and buckets of water after they were done playing golf and sitting on the patio. He wanted to round up a bunch of guys from around town to help. We came up with a plan to stage people on the roof with several buckets of water and others with water guns to come in from every possible escape route and drench every one of the women that were there that night. Together, we rounded up the troops and set the plan in motion. It worked perfectly. As people ran onto the deck blasting the women with water, the women were all scrambling and trying to find safety. Wherever they ran, they were met with buckets of water or waves of water from water guns. Most of the women were ok with it—several of the women ended up getting back at us, and the whole thing turned into a several-hour-long water fight. This night was a great example of the great atmosphere and fun that was had in Nanton. It was a special place.

I can't talk about Nanton without talking about its passion for scramble golf. Scrambles were the rage in Southern Alberta, and we hosted the biggest of them all at Nanton. Every year, the men's scramble had 328 players. No, that's not a typo. One year, I remember we had over 50 teams on the waiting list. If we had had space on the course, we could've hosted well over 500 players. Gambling, drinking, sandbagging, a comedy show, tons of prizes, and of course—golf, made for a wild weekend every year. The number of hours I put into that weekend is something I could no longer do at my advanced age, but it was so awesome. Golfers in Southern Alberta looked forward to the event every year.

In my first three years at Nanton, the Food & Beverage operation was leased to private companies to run. The company that held the lease that third year did not work well at all. Honestly, it was a disaster. The members and guests of Nanton Golf Club were not taken care of in the way I would have wanted them to be on this side of the operation. It negatively impacted the club in a big way. Much of the heartache and headache from the situation fell on me. All of the complaints, the member events, or company tournaments upset with the quality of the food and services they received made for a tough year for the club and myself. The problem was, there was nothing I could do to fix it. The contract was leased to a private business where I had no authority. I suggested to the board of directors that a good solution would be leasing the Food & Beverage contract to me.

What did I know about running a restaurant? Nothing. I knew that I liked going to restaurants and enjoyed eating at them. I knew how to run a business and I knew about customer service and marketing. I knew what the members and guests wanted and expected, and I felt that I could find a way to deliver it. The board agreed. For my last nine years at Nanton, the Food & Beverage operations were my business, which worked out well for both myself and the club. I went from having no clue how to run F&B operations to doing it very successfully now for over 25 years.

Before Nanton, the other clubs I had worked at were privately owned facilities. Nanton was my first and only experience working with a board of directors in the golf world. There's no question that in many scenarios, this can be exceedingly difficult. Over the years, I've fielded many phone calls from peers in the industry looking for feedback and advice on how to deal with boards. Generally, I feel that the hearts of most board members are in the right place, and many of them are successful in their own chosen careers. The board of directors plays an important role in protecting the interests of the club. However, they are not experts in running a golf course like the people they hire.

At Nanton, I was extremely fortunate to work with boards that I felt recognized my skill set and let me do what I needed to do. Certainly, there were times when I did not agree with what the board wanted or dealt with board members that could make my job more difficult. Ultimately, dealing with different board members over the years was positive for me, and over time, we accomplished many wonderful things. One of those things was allowing me to run the Food & Beverage operations at Nanton. My greatest feedback on working with a board is that you need to be good at building relationships with people. If you're doing an excellent job and have the best interests of the business top of mind in decision-making, then dealing with a board should go well.

What made me leave a place that I enjoyed so much and was passionate about for 12 years? It started with my contract negotiations after 11 years. The facilities at Nanton were old and needed replacement. They weren't big enough or suitable for the volume of business we were doing. It was time for something to be done.

I was in discussions and negotiations with the board on staying in Nanton forever as the head professional/manager of the club and keeping the Food & Beverage operations as my own business. In return for such a lengthy commitment on both sides, I was willing to pay for 50 percent of a new clubhouse, knowing that I would get that money back several times over through the Food

& Beverage operations in the future. As word filtered out to others in the community about these discussions, some of the feedback was that the club should be making the profits from F&B rather than me. This led to discussions of a 10-year deal. At that point, I was no longer interested in contributing any money to a new building. I ultimately signed a 5-year agreement to continue running F&B and the club.

In the golf world, this is still a solid commitment, but something didn't sit right with me. I wasn't comfortable hearing the feedback that people thought the club should consider taking over the F&B to make money for the club. I felt that could be a huge issue in the future and my next negotiation. The F&B was extremely profitable and something I didn't want to lose at Nanton. I also missed being in the Edmonton area and I was tired of missing so many family functions. I started thinking that the time was right for me to move back to Edmonton for the right opportunity. That opportunity came a year later: I was offered the role of General Manager/Executive Golf Professional at The Ranch Golf Club in Edmonton. But more on that later.

The Nanton Golf Club and the community

is a truly special place. I enjoyed my time there, and I have so many great memories. If I have one regret, it's that I never really had the opportunity for a proper goodbye. I've been back a few times to play golf over the years, and several members have reached out and played at The Ranch or stopped by for a visit. Those visits are always appreciated.

Once a Bison, Always a Bison

Besides golf, I have another huge passion: hockey. During most of my time at Nanton Golf Club, I was also the general manager of the Okotoks Bisons Junior Hockey Club. You're probably wondering how my time volunteering with a hockey team is relevant to my journey, my career, and my business perspective. Well, let me tell you more about it!

The Bisons Junior Hockey Club is incredibly special to me. From 1996 to 2006, I gave so much time (11 years!) and energy to it, and I turned the team into a juggernaut in Junior Hockey. I used many of the same skills that I use to operate a business: hard work, dedication, passion, and creating a culture where people want to be part of the team. The Bisons are part of the Heritage Junior Hockey League, which has teams from all over Southern Alberta (excluding Calgary). There's also a Northwestern Alberta Junior Hockey League and a Northeast Alberta Junior Hockey League. There was a Calgary Junior Hockey League that only had teams from Calgary—eight teams total. The Edmonton teams were part of the Capital Junior Hockey League, which had five Edmonton teams plus teams from the surrounding towns close to Edmonton. In total, there are about 50 Junior B teams in Alberta.

It all started while I was working a golf show at a high school in Okotoks. I was there on behalf of Nanton Golf Club to sell merchandise and promote the course. A man named Dennis Hatt stopped by to visit and talk golf, but we ended up talking about hockey more than anything else. Dennis worked in banking, but he also mentioned that he was the general manager of the Foothills Bisons Junior Hockey Club (later became known as the Okotoks Bisons).

At the time, they were playing in the Heritage Junior Hockey League Championship against the Stettler Lightning—my hometown. I was planning to attend the game after the golf show. Dennis rolled out the red carpet for me at the game and I continued going to games the next season as a fan and as a friend to Dennis. Before long, I was helping out the team and traveling to some road games.

One day, Dennis shared that he was being transferred to Lethbridge for work. He needed me to take over additional duties for the hockey club and become interim general manager. That year, the Bisons won the Heritage Junior Hockey League championship (their home league) and went on to the Provincial Championships—I went along, too. Shortly after that season, the board of directors appointed me as the new general manager of the Bisons Junior Hockey Club.

During my time with the Bisons, our regular season record included 339 wins and only 56 losses. We won many league championships and trips to the Provincial Championships winning multiple silver and bronze medals that I still proudly display in my basement. My biggest on-ice accomplishment was going to six consecutive Provincial Championships: 2001, 2002, 2003,

2004, 2005, and 2006. We never did win the Provincial title, which is still my biggest regret. In fact, many called it the "Murray Curse." I don't think it's a real thing, but many others called it that.

In junior hockey, as players age out (players must be 21 years old or younger to be eligible), teams generally rise to the top and then fall off. We never did. Each year, I would recruit a new group of rising young stars to replace the guys that graduated or moved on. We continued our success over the long haul. I will always believe that we were the best team in Alberta several of the years we went to provincials, but couldn't win the big title everyone thought we would. For example, one year we had a dominant team the entire season. But at the Provincial Championships in Grand Prairie, a smaller city in northern Alberta, everyone expected the Edmonton River Kings to win, as they were the defending Western Canadian Champions. We went through the round-robin undefeated, including beating the Edmonton Royals (they were swept by the River Kings in the Capital Junior Hockey League final). We played the River Kings in the semifinal and won, which set up a rematch with the Edmonton Royals in the final. Somehow, we lost that game.

Another year, we were dominant all season. We swept every team in the playoffs, including Red Deer in the league final. We were 5-0 against Red Deer during the regular season and playoffs. In provincials, we went through the round-robin undefeated and came up against Red Deer in the semifinal. We outshot them in the game—triple the shots on goal compared to what they put up. We lost in double-overtime, and Red Deer ended up winning the Provincial and Western Canadian championships. The Murray Curse struck again! I believe part of the issue was that we were so good for many years with little adversity during the regular season or playoffs. When we met adversity in some provincials, our lack of experience with it showed and we didn't know how to deal with it.

Early on with the Bisons, there were two memorable moments that made me put in the time and effort to create the winning culture that we had. The first year, when I was coming back from the Provincial Championships as interim GM, we had a goalie named Trent Rieger. He was in his final year of eligibility with the team.

When we arrived at the dressing room back in Okotoks after Provincials, he was officially done playing with the Bisons. I finished getting everything put away and got ready to lock up. I did one final check of the dressing room and I found Trent sitting in his locker stall with tears streaming down his face. I can't remember how long we stayed together in the dressing room talking and reminiscing about his career with the Bisons. But I do remember recognizing and learning in that moment how important the Bisons organization was to Trent on and off the ice. I knew that I needed to carry on the Bison traditions and do what I could to create memories and experiences that would last a lifetime for players and their families.

The second big moment happened at the end of the 1997-1998 season. Our regular season was the worst on record during my time as general manager, with 25 wins and 12 losses. Comparatively, our best season record during my time as general manager was 36 wins and one loss in my final season, and five of the years I was GM we had three losses or less. The Bisons were a good team that season but suffered a few key injuries late in the year that made a championship unlikely. We lost in the South Division final to our biggest rival in the league. In the handshake lineup at the end of the series, my peer from the other team said something to me that shook me to the core. It was disrespectful to me, our organization, and our players. Although I'm a calm and laid-back person, that moment ramped up my intensity around hockey for most of the next decade. I used that degrading comment as fuel for the rest of my career with the Bisons. I never wanted to lose to that person or that team again. I came pretty close to achieving that goal. We only lost to the other team one year in the playoffs and occasionally a game here and there in the regular season over my remaining tenure with the team.

A couple of key phrases that we used day in and day out were: "Heart, Pride, Sacrifice." These three characteristics are so important to be successful both in sports and in business. The second was, "You get what you give." The more effort you put in, the more rewarding it will be for you. These are qualities that the players in our program could take into their everyday lives and careers. Their time with the Bisons taught them well and the success they achieved in hockey helped them grow as people.

When I decided to search for a job in Edmonton, I knew I had to step down from my post as general manager of the Bisons Junior Hockey Club. Saying goodbye to the organization and "my boys" was one of the hardest things I've ever done in my life. After I stepped down, the Okotoks newspaper wrote that the culture I created led to remarkable success for the organization. Local sportswriter Ryan Laverty wrote:

> *In all my years covering sports, I can honestly say I have never come across a more committed, more passionate community volunteer than the guy affectionately known as the Murr-man. McCourt never lied about his agenda, never made excuses for trying to ice the best team he could year in, year out, but his commitment to excellence did more than rub off on his teams; it defined them.*

The Bisons' Team President, Jay Pritchard, said:

> *Some people are blessed with the ability to cause others to be great. When I think of*

> the word 'volunteer,' I think of someone who gives at the highest level because he wants to. Put those two [ideas] together, and you have Murray McCourt. For 11 years, he has given himself to this team and because of that, there are hundreds of young men out there who have learned what it is to be a leader.

And lastly, superstar player Jordy Ferguson said:

> I came back every year to play for a man that I respected and loved, and who had a passion and dedication to the game that made me want to win for him. What I will not ever forget is how proud I am to be a Bison, the friends I have made, the laughter and the tears that were shared, and—you—Murray. Thanks for everything, it's been a great ride.

That time in my life is filled with so many incredible memories. Once a Bison, always a Bison!

You are What You Eat

Similar to my time with the Bisons Junior Hockey Club, you may be wondering why I'd pause to write about health and fitness. However, many habits and business strategies go hand-in-hand with health. Being successful in business requires hard work, dedication, and patience. These same traits are vital for success in your health and fitness journey.

When I was growing up, I had to have been one of the pickiest eaters in the world. When I tell people the small list of things I would eat, it's embarrassing: meat, cheese, bread, pasta without sauce, french fries, corn, candy, cake—that is it. Fruits and vegetables did not stand a chance. And I didn't grow out of this stage like many young kids do. I usually skipped breakfast, and then would have a steak sandwich and fries for lunch, followed by a big plate of spaghetti smothered in butter and parmesan cheese for dinner. It was a horrendous cycle, and I didn't start eating healthy until I was in my mid-30s. I'm getting payback now as my son is an incredibly picky eater. I hope he changes much sooner than I did. It took some health issues to help me see that I needed to improve my eating habits.

During my school years, I was active in sports, and of course walked the golf course many times every day while carrying my clubs, which helped my fitness level. Despite my active lifestyle, my eating habits were putting me overweight through most of those years. I did thin out after high school and into my early 20s. I was happy about my weight and how I looked. But I clearly remember when things started to change.

A company hired me to travel to British Columbia, a neighboring province, for a couple of weeks to market and sell their new product with another assistant professional. Off I went, staying in hotels and eating all my meals in restaurants. None of it was special—but I didn't make healthy choices. When I returned home, my size-34 pants were too tight, and I needed to go buy a bigger size. This began a period of me not treating my body well for an awfully long time. Golf is a social sport, after all.

My lifestyle became eating meals mostly at restaurants. If I dined out, I would have chicken wings as an appetizer, a steak sandwich for my meal, and usually a slice of cake for dessert. Nanton Golf Club was an extremely social community, and I often had drinks on the course and at meals. Over the years, my pant size grew until I was wearing size 40 and topped out at just over 250 pounds. This unhealthy lifestyle led to health issues, including high cholesterol. My doctor told me that if I didn't make meaningful changes, I may not live to see age 40. I knew things had to change!

It took a lot of time and work, but slowly, I did change how I eat. Although I didn't have much variety in my food choices, and fruits and vegetables were not overly appealing, I started to try a few things here and there and found healthy foods that I could eat. I've even learned to eat and like several vegetables! It took many years, but since my mid-40s, I have eaten a healthy, balanced diet and I find ways to get fruits and vegetables into my daily meals. Now, I do eat breakfast, which is a smoothie made with fruit, spinach, and protein powder. Supper is generally some kind of protein with rice or potatoes and a vegetable. My go-to snack is either a protein shake with fruit or a protein shake with greens. I would still call myself a picky eater, but not anything close to what I was like most of my childhood or adult life up to that point.

Unlike eating healthier, I was eager to start exercising. Over the years, I've done many activities, including boot camps and a lot of yoga early in my health journey. I was a big runner for several years, too. I had plans to complete a half marathon, with the goal of receiving a medal. That never happened, but I've run many half-marathons on my own, just not an official race. Then, I started lifting weights and cutting back on the running. Now, I have a good balance between weightlifting and running to help me achieve my goals.

As I changed my diet and exercised consistently, my health improved. My pant size dropped, and the doctor visits yielded better results, confirming that I was on a much better path. I learned over time that the phrase, "You can't outwork a bad diet," is an accurate statement. Despite my best efforts, I wasn't satisfied with my results. I worked with personal trainers and dietitians to figure things out, and it all pointed back to nutrition. I've been tracking what I put into my body for about a decade, and now fully I understand the importance of the phrase, "You are what you eat." It's so true, and my health journey is a testament to that statement.

I've also realized that I'll likely never be completely satisfied with how I look, no matter how much I work out or what I eat. Today, I consider myself healthy. There are zero issues at my annual physicals. I've been back in a size-34 pant size for several years. I'm as strong as I've ever been and can still run a half-marathon if I want. All of these results took a ton of hard work and lots of patience. Nothing happens overnight. It was a huge lifestyle change at first but now it's one that I choose.

In the winter months, I work out for one to two hours every day between lifting weights, cardio, and stretching. This is cut down in the summer when I'm busier, but I do walk and carry my clubs most rounds that I play golf. I watch what I eat very closely, and my alcohol intake is significantly reduced. Now I only drink red wine. The difference in how I feel and the energy I have now is so much different than when I was much younger. The hard work, dedication, and patience have paid off, and my journey to better health has been successful!

Elevating the Food & Beverage Experience at Your Golf Club

Offering great value is a key element to the success of any Food & Beverage (F&B) operation. For golf clubs, F&B operations can and should be a big profit center. Think about it: at a typical golf club, there are tons of opportunities to create revenue from F&B sales throughout the day. This starts first and foremost at the restaurant, where golfers may pick up an early morning coffee, or at lunch, where they grab a hot dog and a bag of chips at the turn. It continues on the golf course itself, where a beverage cart often roams the course offering refreshments to players. More opportunities arise in the afternoon and evening as players stick around for a meal or cocktail postgame play at the patio or the bar.

However, for many clubs, having profitable F&B operations is a challenge. There are multiple types of cuisine available, from grab-and-go options like a sandwich to a higher-end, sit-down, multi-course meal. Additionally, time is a big factor in whether or not a sale is made. For example, if a player shows up late and has a limited time before beginning their round, he or she probably won't order an entree that might take 20 minutes to prepare. And if the sandwiches and other prepared meals are gone, it could cost you another sale. Great customer service and hospitality are also in high demand.

If the F&B program is not managed properly, it can be a financial drain on overall operations and will ultimately cause a club to lose profits. One time, I was playing a PGA of Alberta event at a club, and when the round ended, they offered two lunch specials. Most players that stuck around, including me, were talking about how terrible the food was. The issue was obvious—they were using extremely low-quality products. There is a niche for restaurants who do this and charge accordingly. However, if I'm in a restaurant and see a steak sandwich on special for a super low price, I won't order it because I know I won't be happy with the quality. This approach doesn't work at a golf course. You don't want everyone sitting around talking about how much they do not enjoy their meal—it's a bad impression and leaves a bad taste in the mouth.

Great F&B programs start with friendly service and a welcoming atmosphere. Is your restaurant and patio clean and organized? Is your staff dressed well? Are they alert and smiling? Ensure that your team is friendly and outgoing, and warmly greets each table shortly after everyone sits down. Make sure that your staff's phones are silent and out of sight, ideally in the break room or secured away in a locker. This is the starting point and the foundation for success.

When selecting staff, my philosophy is that I'm always looking to hire the best people that I can. Their experience is not as important as their great personality and positive attitude, which give the type of service that I want to provide to guests. If great people apply and they happen to have experience in the department they want to work in, that's a bonus. Training starts with our staff orientation each year. In great detail, I review who we are as a business, the three pillars of our success, and lay out expectations. I expect our staff to do all they can each and every day to ensure that guests receive a fantastic experience.

The hours that your restaurant is open should correlate and be longer than you have tee times booked. If you aren't open, you can't make sales. Having your Food & Beverage operations open is part of the service that is expected by guests and you can't pass up opportunities to make revenue. You need to ensure that golfers with early tee times can come in and get a coffee and a bite to eat if they desire. The restaurant and kitchen should also stay open until after the last golfer leaves the property. Not having food and beverage service offered will upset the customers and take away from their overall experience that day. If a customer doesn't have a great F&B experience on their first visit, it's likely they will make other plans to eat before or after their round on their next visit.

Overall food quality is extremely important at a golf course. People have expectations for food service when they go out, and even higher meal expectations at a golf course. Golf isn't a cheap sport to play, and when you're dining at a golf course, it's reasonable to expect a higher quality of food. This includes taste, presentation, and service. If your golf facility is lacking in any three of these areas, I recommend making changes to your food and beverage offerings. You don't need to provide premium food like at a five-star fine dining restaurant, but you do want golfers to walk away feeling like the food was just as great as their round of golf. In short, the food and beverage portion of their day shouldn't lessen their overall experience at your golf course.

Product selection is another key component that ensures you are serving quality products that fit into the price point where you need to be. I remember playing an event at Jasper Park Lodge Golf Club, and I ordered the house wine with my meal after the round. It was a nice surprise, as most golf courses don't serve such a wonderful wine—one that I now drink regularly. I recommend targeting your 10-12 highest-volume food items and spending lots of time with your sales rep and their vendors. Sample a wide variety of options available for these highly-used items. Invite other members of your staff to a taste test and get their opinions too. Remember, it's their job to sell the items on the menu. If they like something, it's easier to sell it. Doing this due diligence will ensure you're making the best choices possible to impress your guests with quality food. If your guests feel that they are receiving quality food at a fair price, this will almost guarantee that they choose to dine in the restaurant during future visits. Ensuring that your pricing is competitive with local restaurants is another important detail for helping golfers choose to dine at your course. Additionally, this helps to create a culture of teamwork by involving your entire staff in these important decisions.

As far as a restaurant menu goes, be sure to include some unique offerings. Personally, I don't think it needs to be overly fancy. For example, maybe tomorrow's special is a bison burger with smoked gouda cheese and dry-aged bacon on a pretzel bun with a side salad and homemade dressing. No matter what type of facility you have, the majority of golfers still want to enjoy pub-style food after their round. It's also important to stay current with industry trends. For a while at The Ranch, we offered a BBQ section on our menu and created our own branded BBQ sauce. It was highly successful the first few years that we did it. Don't forget to track the sales of each menu item and do a full menu analysis on a yearly basis. If any items fall out of favor with guests, we replace them with new, trendy items that we feel our customers would savor.

Use local suppliers when it makes sense for produce, protein, spirits, and other items. The landscape for beer, wine, and spirits has changed significantly in recent years, too. Staying alert to these changes and trends is imperative because it ensures you are offering options that your guests want to enjoy. At The Ranch, we worked with a local brewery and branded our own beer, "Red Wheel," which played off the course's namesake. The beer is extremely popular and customers know and appreciate that it's brewed locally.

Beyond the high-quality food, it's always a good idea to have other ways of attracting guests to come into your restaurant before or after their round. Running nightly specials, like Wing Night, Wine Night, or Trivia Night, is a great strategy for helping people choose to eat at your restaurant. Once they make that choice, you can upsell them with other options that elevate their experience and increase your sales. Food vouchers as part of green fees have become another trend that entices players to spend their dollars in your restaurant.

At Nanton, we started a Wing Night on Thursdays that became incredibly popular. Our staff would pre-cook hundreds of wings in advance to help with the business surge that came each Thursday. Early in the evening, families would come out to enjoy wings and adult beverages while the kids could enjoy practicing their putting and chipping. Later on, the younger crowd would come out in droves, filling up the restaurant. The facility wasn't conducive to that much business volume, so there was often a lengthy wait time to get a table. And once you had a table, especially later in the evening, it could take an hour to get your wings. But no one cared—no one was in a hurry to eat and run. The Nanton Golf Club became the place to be on Thursday nights.

Outside of the restaurant, beverage cart service is a huge key in my eyes. This is a monumental opportunity to sell more product and grow your profit, but it is also a service that golfers expect and deserve. The beverage cart should be out on the course from the moment alcohol service is allowed until close to the end of play at night. My personal mandate, both at Nanton and now at The Ranch, is that the beverage cart is always out during liquor service times. My expectation is that every guest sees the beverage cart three to four times each round. Anything less than that is unacceptable in my eyes. Generally, the more experienced staff are on the cart, and they know and understand the expectation of this service and its overall importance for the guests' experience. Many courses do not do this, and I believe it is the wrong decision. Golfers are all paying the same green fee, so they all deserve the same service, including on days when the weather is not great. The beverage cart needs to be out on the course giving the guests proper service and helping them enjoy their day.

Darrell MacDonald has always been known in Alberta as the best host of PGA Alberta events. Every event he hosted at the Millwoods Golf Club was always a treat to play. You never knew what to expect for food service there, but you always knew it would be fabulous. One special offering that happened often was complimentary food trucks at the event. Darrell certainly knows how to treat his peers!

All of the things I have mentioned combine to offer what is the biggest key to success: value. Value is about what you charge for products, but it's far more than that. The quality of food, service, and overall experience are also key factors. If your guests feel they are getting great value and a positive experience, they will gladly support you in your food and beverage department.

Never forget that your guests' experience is not just about the golf course. It's about everything they experience from the moment they arrive until the moment they leave. Food & Beverage is a huge part of the guest experience so it needs proper attention to ensure your guests have a great day!

Life at The Ranch

After signing the 5-year agreement at Nanton, I immediately started looking for opportunities in Edmonton that off-season. Although there were many open positions on the PGA website, there was only one job that I really wanted: General Manager and Executive Golf Professional at The Ranch Golf & Country Club. Previously, The Ranch, as it's nicknamed, had ranked in the Top 100 courses in Canada and had hosted four Canadian Tour events. I loved the fact that such a highly regarded course was located on the outskirts of Edmonton. I applied. Spoiler alert: I was offered a position at The Ranch that first year that I began looking for a new role, but ended up missing out on the opportunity. One year later, I did land the role. What happened, you ask?

I interviewed for the general manager position at The Ranch but did not think that they were going to offer me the role. I had planned a trip to the Dominican Republic and left for vacation without telling any of my contacts at The Ranch that I was going to be out of town. In this era, cell phones weren't important and I didn't take mine with me on the trip. I left it at home and spent the week far away and completely disconnected.

When I returned, I had several voicemails from The Ranch offering me the job. I contacted them the morning after I returned from vacation. They assumed that I didn't want the position since I hadn't responded to them, and they had started discussions with another candidate. I missed the opportunity because I didn't take my cell phone on vacation. I was heartbroken, but I still had my job at Nanton Golf Club, so ultimately it wasn't that big of a deal.

Later that year, right before Christmas, I heard a rumor that the person who had taken the position at The Ranch left for an opportunity in British Columbia. I phoned one of the owners who I'd met the previous winter and let him know that I was interested in the job and available. He indicated that the official posting was happening the next day, and he wanted me to send my resume to a different owner who would be listed on the posting as soon as possible. I did what he asked, and I received a phone call from the owner listed on the posting later that day, which basically turned into a mini-interview. The next day, the owner from the posting called me again and told me that he wanted me to meet him at The Ranch in early January to get started. I asked, "Does this mean I have the job?" He replied, "Yes."

I was now working as the General Manager and Executive Golf Professional at a golf course that at one time ranked among the Top 100 courses in Canada. I couldn't have been prouder or more excited to get going! Prior to starting as the new general manager, I'd been on property at The Ranch a couple of times to play the course back when I was an Assistant Professional. I didn't remember much about it, but a few holes were pretty memorable, and I looked forward to playing the course again.

Once I started working, some of my enthusiasm was quickly tempered. The clubhouse hadn't been updated in a long time. There were six or seven different carpets throughout the building and even more distinct colors of paint. The furniture was worn out and dated. I found out that the Food & Beverage department ran as a cafeteria without table service; the "snack shack" was the clubhouse and the servers never left their spot behind the counter. I learned that the preferred selection of product was extremely low-quality food. When the snow melted, I noticed the driving range mats were old with the edges all turned up. The ninth green hadn't come through winter well, and the 18th green was completely dead from a trial with a new tarp. There were major issues with all the batteries in the power carts. To be honest, everything was a hot mess.

 I had no clue that there were going to be so many issues and problems when I accepted the role, and it was clear that I had a lot of challenging work ahead of me. Although cleanup on the business side had started the previous year, there was still so much to do. What I did know and did recognize was the deep potential for The Ranch. It was going to be amazing, and I was pumped to take on the challenge of turning it around.

Being so new at The Ranch, I had yet to establish myself with the ownership group. I prioritized projects based on factors such as cost, return on investment, and guest experience. The course was not nearly as profitable back then as it is now, so making improvements took some strategic planning. Early on, I had to communicate more frequently with the owners to get their thoughts and opinions on my ideas. However, I was able to make significant changes in the first couple of years, and we continue to make improvements to both the course and facilities each year.

One major improvement we made early on was adding a snack shack. All of the food and beverage service at the turn was done through the clubhouse. This did not enable staff to offer table service for guests that dined after play, which I found unacceptable. I needed to get a snack shack built on the 10th tee to take the workload off the staff in the clubhouse. This strategic move allowed the staff in the restaurant to offer excellent table service. At the time, building the snack shack I wanted to build felt expensive and something that I didn't think I could convince owners to spend money on at that time. I proposed we connect with a local high school to build it, and that worked. I reached out to a local shop teacher and the students in his class built the snack shack for us. After a few years of increased food and beverage operations, we ended up building the snack shack that I felt was required to give guests the best service they could receive.

As I described in Chapter 4, the people you surround yourself with are so important to the success of your organization. I was fortunate to inherit two incredible people at The Ranch who have helped our team achieve everything that we have at the club. Derek Senkow was our young, fiery golf course superintendent. Earlier in his life, he was a point-a-game player in the Western Hockey League, so we already had a common interest. Derek knows the property inside and out. He was talented beyond his years in his management of the turf at The Ranch. He is very passionate about his job and very loyal to The Ranch. There are so many things about Derek that made me excited to work with him.

The Ranch had fired the previous head pro

at The Ranch and strongly encouraged me to elevate a long-time assistant professional at the club to the position. I knew from experience that having someone familiar with the course in that position would be a major benefit to me. The first time I met Shaun Piercey, we had an instant connection. His love of golf and sports matched mine, and I intuitively knew this would be a great fit at The Ranch. Shaun hadn't had much opportunity to get involved in a ton of aspects that he would need to as the head professional, but I knew with my background, it would be easy to guide him in the areas he had yet to learn. Shaun's passion and dedication to The Ranch is so deep and he was the perfect fit for the position. Derek and Shaun still hold the same positions today and are an integral part of all we do at The Ranch. It took more time to find the perfect pieces in other key management positions that I inherited. With our superintendent and head professional in place, we were able to make significant improvements rather quickly.

When I started at The Ranch, I initially signed a two-year agreement. At the end of the first year, I was asked if I would rip up the agreement and sign a longer-term deal. I agreed and signed a three-year deal. At the end of the first year of that agreement, I was asked if I would rip up the deal and sign a longer deal. I agreed and signed a 4-year deal. Things were obviously going very well. After the first year of that agreement, an offer came my way that was simply incredible. There were some changes that were going to happen with the ownership group and as part of that, I was asked if I would agree to sign an agreement that would keep me at The Ranch forever. This offer included me becoming one of the owners of the course. The Ranch had already become my next big passion, and this offer was an incredible opportunity for me. I knew that I would be the general manager/executive professional at my pride and joy, The Ranch, for the rest of my career.

Sunday Matches

When I first started at The Ranch, one of my big marketing priorities was getting tied in with the Edmonton Oilers and the Edmonton Elks (previously Eskimos). I wanted the players of the teams to play golf at The Ranch and share their experiences on social media. My hope was that if people saw celebrities playing golf at The Ranch at the same time that they were playing, or if they just saw a post about it on social media, maybe more guests would play the course. If The Ranch was the exclusive place where athletes from the Oilers and Elks played golf, it would elevate our brand and help make The Ranch a must-visit golf course destination.

It all started when I reconnected with J.J.

Hebert, one of my former hockey players from the Bisons Junior Hockey Club. J.J. was in Edmonton and held a senior position with the Edmonton Oilers communications and media team. He worked closely with the local media and he worked even closer with the players. He often traveled with the team when they were on the road. He started connecting me with players and members of the sports media that liked to play golf. Things snowballed as the initial contacts from J.J. would connect me to more and more people in the sports world. Before long, I was extremely well-connected with much of the sports media in Edmonton and many of the players, coaches, and staff on the Oilers, Elks, and the Edmonton Rush (former National Lacrosse League team). My plan had worked!

When I created this marketing strategy, I didn't know that these connections would lead to many lifelong friendships. With the Elks, the first person that I became good friends with was Kamau Peterson. KP, as he was known, wasn't the best golfer, but he sure loved the game. Through him, I met many other Elks players. Golf was an important topic in the team's dressing room and they were pretty serious about it.

When we played golf together, the players made sure everyone followed the rules, and no putts were ever given. One day, I played 36 holes with KP, Andrew Nowacki, and Ricky Ray—first at the Royal Mayfair and then at the Edmonton Country Club in the afternoon. I was riding a cart with Ricky, and on one hole, he hit his ball a bit left into the trees. KP and "Wack" (Nowacki) both hit theirs a mile right. When we got to Ricky's ball, it sat on a tree root. There was no way I would have hit the ball where it was, unless I was in a tournament. And I knew Ricky didn't want to hit it off the tree root. I'd been a huge Elks fan since I was a kid, and there was no way I could have lived with myself if Ricky had swung and hurt himself. So, I walked up to the ball and kicked it off the tree root. However, I didn't hear the others pull up behind us in their cart. They started yelling at me for improving his lie. Ricky just walked up beside me and said, "Thanks Mur Man."

I was also good friends with Michael Reilly, who was the star quarterback of the Edmonton Elks. He wasn't a great golfer either, but man could he hit the golf ball—really, really far! As far as anyone I'd ever played with. He was a strong and powerful guy. When we played golf together, Mike would always bring a football with him. When we had time waiting on the tee box, I would run patterns and play catch with Mike on the course. It was super cool!

Ryan King was one of the ring leaders of all of the golf games and we played together quite often. He would ensure that all of the golfers that came to the Elks would connect with me. This is a habit he's carried on through his retirement. Not as many of the current players are into golf as in previous years, but Sergio Castillo and a few others still carry on the tradition of Elks players playing golf at The Ranch.

I often get asked who were the best golfers among the Eskimos players. Although Ricky Ray and Noel Prefontaine were solid golfers, I believe that the two best golfers were Matt Nichols and Kelly Malveaux. Matt was a long ball hitter and he even created his own Twitter hashtag #bubba-long, though Mike Reilly could hit his ball further. Matt could play well and mostly shot in the low 70s. Kelly was such a competitor. He loved to gamble, and he had the game to back it up. He was a great ball striker and has my vote as the best golfer of the Elks players over the years.

When J.J. was still with the Oilers, he and his friends and co-workers, Pat Garland and Steve Lines, would connect me with Oilers players that wanted to play golf. Often, J.J., Pat, and Steve would bring players out, as they were big golfers too. Sometimes, I'd get invited to play as well. Over the years, I became good friends with a few of the players, including Jason Strudwick and Zack Stortini. Zack was a great guy and he loved to play golf. We would sometimes go to Edmonton Rush games together, and Zach was very recognizable, so kids would line up to get his autograph. I'd stand off to the side waiting for him—he wouldn't go anywhere until he'd signed for everyone that wanted an autograph. He was a great ambassador for the team and for Edmonton. Over the years, Jason Strudwick and I played many games of golf and attended Elks games together with our families. Jason and his wife, Schoena, also came to Jessica and my wedding.

More recently, I've become good friends with Oilers goalie Stuart Skinner. He takes golf pretty seriously and puts in lots of time and effort to improve his game, though becoming a new dad may change that. He is also one of the nicest guys you will ever meet, and there is no question in my mind that he has an exceptionally long and successful NHL career ahead of him.

In my first year at The Ranch, I started booking tee times every Sunday morning at 11 a.m. I would invite local sports players or media personnel to play. I generally had between four and eight guys play each week. This became known over time as the "Sunday Match." It has evolved over the years, especially the past few years as most of the Oilers and Elks players don't stick around the city in the offseason. The one staple over the years has been Kevin Karius from Global Sports. He was invited one Sunday by Jason Gregor from TSN 1260. Kevin and I hit it off and have been great friends for around 15 years now. Kevin ended up helping me organize the Sunday matches over the years and together, we would figure out who to invite. As the players stopped staying in the city, we built a regular foursome that lasted several years. Kevin and I played with Eskimos legend Danny Kepley every Sunday, and we would invite one other person to join us. Danny and I became very close friends and listening to his stories from his career was fascinating to hear for a long-time Elks fan. But eventually, Danny ended up moving back to the United States. Over the past couple of years, Kevin and I have played with our head professional, Shaun Piercey, and events manager, Adam Wisser, from The Ranch. Kevin and I have always played season long matches where the loser would have to invite the winner and their spouse over to their house for a fancy home-cooked dinner. Shaun and Adam now participate in those matches against Kevin as well. It makes for a great excuse to get together away from the course and, to be honest, the dinners are almost always at the Karius household.

My plan of generating interest in The Ranch from others was certainly working. People would book tee times around 11 a.m. every Sunday just so they could see who would be playing. I would always see people bringing out their phones to take pictures and text their friends about who they were seeing play golf at The Ranch. It's been a lot of fun getting to know so many people in the sports world. It's provided so many benefits to The Ranch and some incredible friendships and memories for me.

Part Two
The Back Nine
Business Lessons Learned

The Layers of Your Brand

Now that you know my golf story, I want to spend the rest of this book talking about business. Operating a successful, profitable business takes a lot of hard work, passion, dedication, and time. It's important to know exactly who you are and strive to emanate that every day, which takes years of practice. In the age of social media and digital communication, building and maintaining an active online presence is also imperative. Having a supportive group of people around you helps too.

All of the business principles that I'll be sharing with you can be applied to any type of business. Whether you want to run your own restaurant, start a marketing firm, or oversee a successful real estate agency, each of the concepts we discuss in the chapters ahead will be beneficial to helping you succeed. Everything that's in these chapters has been learned from my personal experience. Some of it was trial and error; some of it was observing and streamlining a process. Let's get started!

At The Ranch, there are a few layers that guide who we are as an organization. The first layer revolves around our three core business pillars. The first pillar is Premier Conditions. We want to offer guests at The Ranch a course that has outstanding conditions every day. From the tee box or the fairway to the green, our goal is to ensure that the course is in outstanding shape on every hole and every dog-legged turn.

Our second pillar is top-notch Customer Service. We want our guests to feel special and appreciated for choosing to play The Ranch. Our team strives to meet and care for every guest's needs throughout the day. From having a positive check-in and friendly interaction with our starter to observing the beverage cart several times on the course to the great hospitality in the newly-branded Red Wheel Pub & Grill following a round, we want guests to receive excellent service. This ensures they have a positive experience at The Ranch.

Our third pillar is that we offer Unmatched Value. The first two pillars clearly play a role in the value that a guest feels that they receive at The Ranch. Playing a course with great conditions and receiving top-notch service provides value. The price that a guest pays to golf and for other services at the club is a huge piece of this. My personal theory is to always charge a fair and reasonable price for what you're offering. We strive to live up to these standards daily and are immensely proud, knowing that we are accomplishing our goals.

The second layer that guides The Ranch is a strategic, laser-focused business model. At one time, The Ranch sold both regular memberships and corporate memberships while also trying to host a large number of corporate events. These things don't exactly go hand-in-hand, and trying to be good in both areas will always lead to not being great at either. Members want access to play; tournaments remove that access. Ultimately, you need to decide which of these items is most important and what aligns with your business model. Ask yourself what you want your golf business model to look like. You can certainly do both; however, if you have members, you'll need to add restrictions around the number of tournaments you can host and when you can host them. This way, the members are aware and can accept the terms or take their membership elsewhere.

At The Ranch, we chose to stop selling regular memberships, with the exception of a few that were grandfathered in. It simply didn't make sense for our business model—we wanted to host as many tournaments as we could, without any limitations or restrictions. Due to that strategic decision, The Ranch is likely the busiest tournament golf course in the province.

The third and final layer that guides The Ranch is knowing who we are as a brand. It's impossible for any business to be all things to all people. A golf course certainly can't cater to the wants and needs of all golfers. For any business, it is imperative to know exactly what your brand is and who you are.

For example, if you go to McDonald's for dinner, do you expect to get a gourmet burger? If you dine at Ruth's Chris Steakhouse, is it reasonable to expect that your meal will only cost $15? These businesses know their brand and deliver exactly what you'd expect by going to each restaurant. They don't stray into the other lane and try to be something they aren't to please a single customer or a group of customers.

Once you *know* who you are, it is then equally important to *be* who you are. The best thing you can do for your business is to stay in your lane. Know your brand, execute it, and repeat. Trying to step outside of who you are as a business and a brand doesn't work. Plus, it can be difficult to properly care for customers if you're trying to be something you aren't. And trust me, people can smell that a mile away. The good news is that there's a market for a wide variety of options in all industries. Whether your business is in the entry-level lane, the high-end market, or somewhere in between, there are customers out there that are looking for what you offer.

Key advantages of knowing your brand include: providing motivation and direction for your staff, enabling customers to know what to expect, representing your promise to your customers, creating recognition and trust, and illustrating your value proposition.

One big area that can impact your brand is the conditions of your golf course. Golfers have extremely high expectations when it comes to golf course conditions. Although some of these expectations can be unrealistic, the condition of your golf course can have a significant impact on your brand, both positive and negative.

People in the golf industry are familiar with and understand the work involved in keeping a golf course in good condition. At times, work needs to be done, like aerating the greens, which negatively impacts the condition of the course in the short-term. However, it's required for the long-term health of the greens. Unfortunately, customers don't always understand this.

The key to having your course conditions positively impact your brand is **consistency over time**. Word will get out about the conditions of all the golf courses around your geographic location. Golf courses that are generally discussed in a positive light around course conditions will see their reputation improve organically by word of mouth. Having great conditions year after year makes golfers in the area feel confident that they can expect great conditions when they choose to play at your facility. It takes time to build the type of reputation that you're looking for. And if, for whatever reason, your course has a bad year, it will take lots of time—perhaps even years—to gain your reputation back. Consistent, positive conditions will help the consumer choose to play at your course over other golf courses that are not building the same positive reputation.

Another area that can affect your brand is the price point of a golf course. While at Fort In View, I started to formulate my own strategy for marketing and pricing—this was part of my trying to set myself apart from others. My philosophy on pricing is to set your price at a fair and reasonable rate so that those playing the course feel like they receive great value. Then, you never discount your pricing! If you set your price properly, there should never be a need to discount it because you're already offering the value that people are looking for. Discounting it from that rate will devalue your product and give people the impression that your course is not likely worth your regular price.

Have I always stuck by my own thoughts on pricing? No. I have tried things over time that went against this philosophy, and I pretty much always regretted the decision after the fact. At times, I have been forced into decisions about pricing. A great example of this is when the COVID-19 pandemic began. We had our pricing strategy set for the year, and I was happy with what was planned. We had designed our pricing around value added for being part of our loyalty app program.

When COVID started, we had to move to online bookings with prepayment. Our system couldn't differentiate if someone booking online had our loyalty app or not, so I decided that everyone would get the lower price. This went against all I believe in, but at that time, I felt like I had no other option. If you are looking to create extra business on soft days of the week or times during the day on your tee sheet, then look to add value rather than discount your price. Give something additional to your customer such as a food voucher or a sleeve of balls—but don't drop your price! Every time I have gone against my own beliefs, for whatever reason, when I realized my mistake—it is very hard to go back from the decision and it will take time to get away from what you are doing and get back to where you should be price-wise.

The price point can and will impact golfer expectations. Just as with all businesses, varying price points deliver different quality golf courses. Wherever a golf course lands in the spectrum, it needs to ensure that course conditions match the price, to avoid lessening the value that guests receive. If a course and its conditions don't live up to the price of play, this can negatively impact the brand. There's no question that being known as one of the best-conditioned courses in your area helps set you apart from the competition. It also helps your brand and the success of your golf business in many ways. It's important to keep that in mind during the budget process to avoid compromising golf course conditions and maintain a strong brand.

No matter where you are, be sure to take the time and go through the process of determining exactly who you are as a brand. Then stay in your lane and be who you are. It's the best way to ensure your path to success.

Over the years, there have been times when we have had to react and evolve to different changes in the world. At one point at The Ranch, on the golf side of things, I'm not sure if we could have done anything to grow our business further. We were doing over 11,000 tournament rounds per year, and our tee sheets were full seven days in advance, which was as far in advance as we open public bookings. But I was looking for other ways to grow our business so that we could keep more staff year-round and become even more profitable.

This led us to stay open in the winter for various events. We offered sleigh rides, fireworks shows, and bonfires. We created an event called the Winter Warrior Challenge, which was an obstacle race in the snow and cold, similar to a Tough Mudder or Spartan race. We branded our own promotional products company that we called "Tough Stuff Promotions." This continues to be a highly successful part of our business. These creative ideas differentiated us from what many other facilities were offering and helped us stay busy in the winter.

In the '90s, the economy took a turn and everything changed. Our tournament business dropped and the tee sheets went from being full seven days in advance to having open tee times on most days. We needed to attract new business. Although the golf course had a great layout and most people enjoyed it, the course was extremely difficult. To help us attract customers that were playing elsewhere due to its challenging nature, we spent several years making the course more user-friendly and enjoyable for golfers at all levels. We tried to keep it difficult for seasoned players but limit the challenges for newer or higher-handicap players. These changes helped the tee sheets fill up again. As the economy improved, the demand for tournaments was rising and were just about back to the levels of busyness we had seen before the economic crash.

    Then, the COVID-19 pandemic happened in 2020. We evolved again as hosting tournaments, the biggest part of our businesses, was canceled for much of two years. We became a daily fee course, which worked out fine as golf was booming. But without our tournament side of the business, our revenues weren't what we were used to seeing. We made it through the other side, and when restrictions were lifted, tournament business boomed again. Getting a tee time at The Ranch was a challenge due to course popularity—but to us, it was back to business as usual.

Another area that The Ranch continues to evolve in is how it engages with customers. We've learned that engaging with customers on social media is pretty powerful. As you may already know, social media is a great way to market your business and grow your brand. Here are a few key reasons why using social media channels is important for your business:

- **Increase brand awareness**—The vast majority of the population in your area use social media. This is where people go to find information and discover what's going on. If everyone else is using this space, you need to as well. You need to be seen and this is the best place to do that.
- **Humanize your brand**—If people see posts of golfers out playing your course and having a great time, or if they see pictures of your course in great condition, this

will trigger them to consider booking their next tee time with you. Seeing is believing. It gives you the opportunity to show potential customers the enjoyment of your current customers. This will lead to business growth.

- **Keeps you top of mind**—Most people check their social media several times daily. Keep your posts interesting and informative. The more people see information from you, the more likely they will think of you next time they go to book a tee time.

- **Boost your sales**—Whether your presence gets people booking tee times with you or your posts are geared towards people spending money in your pro shop or restaurant, your sales will certainly grow with proper social media use.

- **Influencer partnership opportunities**—Word of mouth is one of the best ways to get people to use your products and services. You want to get people talking about your business. Using local influencers (people who have a large social media following) can get more people seeing and learning about your business. If local celebrities are using your business, that may help them make the decision to use your business as well.

- **Customer Engagement**—With traditional media, communication is a one-way street where you are sharing your message with the customer with no way for them to communicate back to you. Social media is different. Your customers or potential customers can reach out to you directly through social media, just as you can with them. If you want your customers to stay engaged, you must be engaged and actively respond to those that communicate with you. If you communicate with your customers in this way, you are sure to see further support from them in the future.

- **Customer Service**—As social media continues to grow, the expectation of your customers is that social media is an acceptable way of communication. They expect you to communicate with them in this way just as they would via email or over the phone. This simply needs to become part of how you communicate with your customers.
- **Monitor Competition**—It's always important to see what your competitors are doing. Following your competitors on social media can help you do that. You will see what they are doing for offers and merchandise launches and see what customers are saying about their experience with them. All great information to know.

One thing that will always remain the same for our team at The Ranch is the continued desire to work to further elevate our brand and find ways to constantly improve what we do and the service we provide. We will always celebrate our successes, but will also analyze our operations to determine if there are better ways to do things to bring greater enjoyment to our guests. Our three pillars will continue to drive how we operate and manage the business in a way that enables us to succeed for many years to come.

Why Value is So Valuable

In your business, are you providing your guests with great value? Does your definition of value align with your guest's definition? For our purposes, "value" can be defined as the benefits and services that a customer feels he or she received in exchange for their payment.

Offering great value is important for your business for several reasons. Great value helps to attract and retain customers. When players get used to consistent, top-notch value at your golf course, this will increase customer loyalty and build your brand reputation. By offering a great golf course with high-quality products in both your pro shop and restaurant at reasonable prices, your business will differentiate itself from competitors and create a positive customer experience.

This rule also applies to the high value that you may offer at your bakery, boutique, gym, or even a roofing company. Great value also improves profitability, no matter what industry your business is in. Customer retention and word-of-mouth advertising can lead to increased sales and revenue over time.

So how do you quantify "great value?" Unfortunately, we can't simply focus on price as the determining factor of value. Although customers do spend their hard-earned money when they invest in products or services, they also "pay" in time, effort, and convenience.

In golf, *time* refers to the duration that a customer spends searching for available tee times, evaluating the quality of the courses, booking the tee time, the duration of the commute to the golf course, and their time spent at the facility. For a different business, let's say a barber shop or salon, for example, a customer's *time* might include evaluating the types of hair services that your shop provides, booking an appointment online, the time driving to the store, and the time spent in the chair.

Effort refers to the mental or physical energy required to make the booking for the tee time. This includes filling out information on an online booking platform. It also includes travel to the golf course. Outside of the golf course, other examples of *effort* may look like filling out a request form with details for a custom cake before meeting the baker or sharing specifics about the custom home addition before meeting with the builder.

Convenience refers to how easy and accessible it is for a customer to find available tee times and make a booking. It also refers to the commute to the course—is it close and convenient or further away and a few extra minutes? This also applies to your business. Is it easy for your customer to contact you? Is your storefront close or far away from their home or place of work? Does your website make it easy or difficult for a customer to find the information they need?

By minimizing the time, effort, and inconvenience associated with the purchase of a product or service, businesses can enhance the overall customer experience and improve customer satisfaction.

Here are some keys to offering great value:

- **Make the value/price ratio seem bigger than it is.** Make customers feel that they are appreciated. Go the extra mile with your service. Consider if there is additional value that you can offer such as a free gift, a loyalty program, reward points, etc.
- **Make your services or products easy to buy.** Is it easy to book tee times online? Can customers book tee times on an app on their phone?
- **Create a unique value proposition.** Make it easy for your customers to see why they should play your course over the competition. What makes you different from everyone else?
- **Work on your brand.** Your company's name itself should be

known for offering value. Develop a consistent method for how you treat your customers, how you deal with issues, how you show hospitality, etc.
- **Provide stellar customer service.** At the end of the day, both your employees and customers are people. Treating them as such can be extremely rewarding for both parties.

Price is always the biggest factor in creating value but it is not the only factor. You must set your pricing fairly and reasonably for what you offer and where you fit in the market. This can be a complex issue, but here are a few ideas to consider:

- **Determine your costs.** Calculate all of the costs associated with producing, marketing, and selling your offerings.
- **Research the market.** Analyze the prices of similar products or services offered by competitors in your industry. Where does what you

offer realistically stack up against your competition? Use this as a ruler for pricing.
- **Other factors.** Take into account economic conditions, supply and demand, supply chain bottlenecks, and any other external factors that could impact pricing.

Ultimately, it's important to strike a balance between being profitable and offering a fair price that provides value to the customer.

In golf, big box stores are competing with pro shops at golf courses for sales. You must keep your pro shop pricing in line with box store pricing so people have the opportunity to choose to support your business. To make the decision easier, entice them with something that provides additional value that a box store can't. When pricing your food and beverage items, you need to be aware of pricing at nearby restaurants to ensure that your pricing does not chase your guests down the road for drinks and dining after play. With your green fee and membership pricing, you must take into account all of the factors listed above. If you can find a way to offer great value and charge less than competitor courses in your area, customers will recognize that and support you.

By offering great value, you are certain to keep your tee sheet full and be more profitable. If there are courses that charge more than you but offer lower quality, that is great for your brand and ensures your business will stay busy.

Another idea to consider is that customers do not necessarily receive the same benefits at your business. Every single customer of yours is different. They come with their own unique experiences and expectations. Their opinion of what makes golf course conditions great will inevitably vary. Some factors include things such as where they normally play, how well or how poorly they play on a particular day, the opinions of their peers, and what the weather was like the day they played your course. This concept can be applied to any business. For example, customers in the construction world appreciate the craft and expertise of a well-known construction team; those eating at a restaurant may enjoy the plating and presentation of a meal; and others love knowing that you are providing outstanding services or repairs.

Please note: it's impossible to meet 100 percent of the expectations of your customers. Some things, like the weather, are out of your control. However, in any business setting, it's important to do all you can each and every day to meet the majority of your customer's expectations. No matter which side of the fence, a guest's experience can have an impact on your business. Customer retention is extremely important and their impressions of their experience will impact how often they support your business in the future. Whether their experience was excellent or downright disappointing, they will share their thoughts with friends and family, or through online reviews. Despite the positive or negative information a customer provides, it still impacts your reputation and can influence whether potential new customers support your business moving forward.

Customer value is the perception of what a product or service is worth to an individual compared to the possible alternatives around them. Value for one customer may not be the same for another customer, which shifts the value either positively or negatively.

Benefits of positive customer value include:

- **Quality of the product or service**—The quality of a golf course can offer value to golfers in several ways: (1) *Enjoyment*: a high-quality golf course that is well-maintained with excellent playing conditions can enhance a golfer's overall experience. Golfers are more likely to enjoy playing on a course with great conditions, which makes it a worthwhile investment of their time, effort, and convenience. (2) *Challenge*: a well-designed course that offers fair and challenging holes adds value. Golfers who feel challenged by a course are more likely to feel that they are receiving great value for their money, as they are provided a stimulating golfing experience. (3) *Amenities*: having quality amenities, including a well-stocked pro shop, a restaurant, and some practice facilities makes golfers feel that they are receiving great value in exchange for their hard-earned dollars. Golfers may be willing to pay more to play a well-known, high-quality course because they are likely to have a positive experience and feel that it is worth the financial investment.

- **Image/Reputation**—The reputation of a golf course is built through several factors: the quality of the course, the level of services provided by the staff, the amenities offered, and the overall experience that a golfer has while at the facility. A golf course that is well-designed and aesthetically pleasing with attractive landscaping, water features, and other amenities has an increased perceived value. This is because a visually appealing course enhances the overall experience for golfers, which makes it more memorable and enjoyable. A positive reputation can lead to an increased demand for tee times, higher prices for green fees, and increased revenue for the course.

- **Experience**—A guest's experience on a golf course can impact their perception of its value in several ways, depending on their individual preferences and expectations. If a guest has an enjoyable experience on the course, they are more likely to perceive it as valuable. The greater the enjoyment of their experience, the higher the perceived value. A challenging golf course may be perceived as more valuable by experienced golfers who enjoy a test of their skills. On the other hand, a less experienced golfer may perceive a difficult course as less valuable if they struggle to play well. A golf course with stunning views and beautiful landscaping may be perceived as high-value by golfers who appreciate the course aesthetics. The secret to an enjoyable experience will depend entirely on the individual.

Offering great value can be a powerful way

for a golf course (or any other business) to differentiate itself from competitors and stand out in the marketplace. It's also a great way to help build a great reputation for businesses. When your golf course or business provides excellent value, it attracts more customers and increases revenue.

Rubbing Shoulders, Shaking Hands

Networking is one of the most important strategies for every business for several reasons. First, networking provides an opportunity to meet new people and develop relationships with potential clients or customers. These connections can lead to new business opportunities and referrals, which can help grow your customer base.

Networking also helps build awareness for your brand. Through networking events and programs, you can promote your business and increase brand visibility. As you meet more people and make new connections, your business will become better known and recognized.

Thirdly, networking can provide access to new resources and information, such as industry insights, market trends, or new technologies. Learning from other business owners and their successes and failures can help you make better decisions for your own business.

Networking also provides opportunities with other business owners and professionals who may have valuable insights, feedback, and advice to share. This feedback can help you improve your business strategy, operations, or product offerings.

Lastly, networking can lead to invaluable partnerships and collaborations with other businesses or organizations. These partnerships can help you expand your reach, access new markets, and create new revenue streams.

With The Ranch just outside the city limits of Edmonton, for many years I had trouble getting trade workers to the course to complete updates and repairs. When the economic downturn occurred in the 2010s, I was looking for opportunities to get repair work done and generate new business for both The Ranch and Tough Stuff Promotions. One day, Shaun, our head professional, walked into my office and told me about a conversation he'd had with one of our ladies league members. She had told him about a networking group called Business Network International (BNI). Based on what Shaun shared, BNI sounded like the solution we needed to solve both problems.

BNI is a networking group where chapters welcome members to their group to work together to grow each other's businesses. The main purpose of BNI is to generate referrals for your business by educating those in your chapter about your business so they can generate sales for you through their network. Each type of business is only allowed one seat in a chapter to ensure there is no competition for similar businesses in the group. For example, each chapter would only allow one realtor, one mortgage broker, one golf course, etc. The group meets weekly and members are encouraged to set up individual meetings with peers in the group to learn more about each other's business. The premise is that you work to educate all other chapter members about your business and provide a brief summary of what you're looking for. Members in turn use their networks to generate referrals for others in their chapter. Often, the referrals turn into business. A goal of most chapters is to refer more than $1 million in business yearly to others in the group, but it's usually much more.

I did my research on BNI and the chapters in the Edmonton area. I ended up targeting the chapter called BNI Premiere because they had a decent number of members and met in a convenient location where I could join. When I reached out to the president at the time, Ben Guitard, he was watching the Masters, and I knew this chapter would be a good fit. After attending a few meetings and going through an interview process, I was an official member of the BNI Premiere networking group.

I retained my BNI membership for close to three years. It was a huge benefit to easily access trade companies and other businesses who happily came to do work at The Ranch. It was a big relief to solve that problem. New business also came to The Ranch. Several new tournaments booked through connections with BNI Premiere. The chapter meetings moved to The Ranch as well. Things were working out very well and the benefits of the amount of time that was invested were crystal clear.

In my second year at BNI, I became president of the chapter. The chapter saw huge growth in membership and closed business, with more than $5 million in referrals to each other that year. At the BNI Awards Gala, our chapter was recognized as Chapter of the Year in BNI Alberta North and I was honored to receive the President of the Year Award.

The following year, I became an ambassador with BNI Alberta North. My role was to train incoming presidents to do their roles and to be a resource for them. I also supported them in growing their chapter. I did all of this on top of being a member of my own chapter. However, there were plenty of benefits, including becoming more well-known in the BNI world, which in turn, helped grow the business.

I met many amazing people in BNI, including Pat Stride, the owner/executive director of BNI Alberta North. Her role in BNI made her deeply connected within the business community and her network was so broad. She was also the owner/executive director of another networking organization, BNI's big brother, which is called Corporate Connections. Unlike BNI, Corporate Connections is designed for owners, CEOs, and general managers of larger companies and businesses. One of the main focus areas of Corporate Connections is to build stronger connections and relationships with peers in your group. These forum groups give you the comfort and trust to share any business struggles you may have. They also give you the opportunity to hear feedback from your peers, as well as experiences and ideas to help you work through any issues. Developing these types of relationships with others generally leads to business growth as well. Building trust with each other leads to opening up your network trying to help each other grow their business. Pat always told me she thought I belonged at Corporate Connections.

Ultimately, I chose to resign from BNI for several reasons. I was clearing my plate of extracurricular activities as the birth of my son was fast approaching. I wanted to focus on The Ranch and my family; with that, some other things had to go. The time spent in my own chapter along with the ambassador work took up more time than I was able to give.

In the fall of 2022, Pat and Hubert Lau, another former BNI member that I knew and respected, approached me to start a new Corporate Connections chapter in Edmonton. Pat wanted to be a member of the chapter and was looking to grow the new chapter with powerful, well-connected business leaders. Hubert and I jumped on board with her, and we are in the midst of growing and building the chapter. The group that we have put together so far is amazing, and it's only the beginning. Great connections have already been made; some have described them as "life-changing." We've had several meetings that make me excited about the opportunities to learn from other members of the group and work together to help each other with business growth. I've learned so much from this incredible group of people and look forward to continued collaborations and the benefits that will certainly happen in the future.

If you're interested in learning more or want to get started, Google "Corporate Connections" or "BNI Chapters in my area." It's a great way to see if this program may be a fit for you and your business. It's also an opportunity to plug into a local chapter.

I'm a huge fan of networking groups and how they can help grow your business. There's no question in my mind that all types of businesses can be highly successful because of their membership in BNI—it's really that powerful. I'm excited to see where things go with our Corporate Connections chapter.

It's always great to grow your network. When you rub shoulders with the right people, you never know what positive outcomes may come from it.

The Power of Innovation

As your golf business continues to grow and change, doing what you've always done won't work forever. Just because something has been done one way for many years doesn't make it the best choice for tomorrow. Your customers will change over time as well. Perhaps your new customer's goals and expectations for their experience at your facility are different from previous or current customers. It's important to always keep your eyes on the future. I don't say this to discourage you, but rather to help you start to think about innovative ways to improve your club or business.

Take a moment and ask yourself:

- *Is my golf course or business staying ahead of the competition?*
- *Is my plan to continue doing what we've done in the past?*
- *Am I willing to evolve and change for the sake of my business?*

Why do club managers and business owners need to be innovative today? Well, for starters, the world has changed significantly over the past few years due to COVID-19. The pandemic and its social, economic, and environmental shifts have made innovation more important than ever. Some of the key reasons include:

- **To stay competitive.** The business landscape is constantly changing. To remain competitive, your business needs to constantly adapt and improve its products, services, and processes. Innovation is the key to staying ahead of the competition and creating unique value propositions that set your business apart.

- **To meet changing customer needs**. Customer needs and preferences are constantly evolving, and your business needs to stay up-to-date with these changes to stay relevant. Innovation can help your business identify and meet these changing needs, whether it's by creating new products or services, improving existing ones, or finding new ways to engage with customers.
- **To increase efficiency and reduce costs**. Innovation can help your business find new and more efficient ways to operate, which reduces costs and improves profitability. For example, implementing new technologies, automating processes, or streamlining operations can all lead to cost savings and increased productivity.
- **To attract and retain top talent**. Innovative companies are often seen as more exciting and attractive places to work, which can

help your business attract and retain top talent. Employees are often drawn to companies that are at the forefront of their industry and offer opportunities for personal and professional growth.

Let's address what it means to be innovative. In simple terms, being innovative is *introducing something new to your business.* It's thinking outside the box, looking past what you feel is currently expected in your business, and finding opportunities to elevate your offerings in the eyes of your customers. To be an innovator, you must constantly seek new ways to change and improve how your business operates. It's important to have a deep understanding of your ideal customer to envision a way to make positive changes.

It's also important to embrace failure during this process. Not everything you seek to implement will work out exactly how you envision it. Some aspects may not work at all, while others will require tweaking and adjustments to get the results you desire. To truly be an innovator, you must embrace lifelong learning. Keeping up with market trends and staying ahead of the curve are two ways to continue learning each day. If you can adapt these ideas, you and your business will both grow.

There are two main areas where you can implement innovation at your current golf facility or business: revenue innovation and your business model.

At The Ranch, we recognized that once there are less than two hours before dark, we stop generating revenue because golfers can no longer complete nine holes safely. We had some internal discussion and brainstorming to try and identify ideas that could help the business generate more revenue later in the day. We wondered if this window of time would appeal to new golfers or families to come out and enjoy golf with a shorter time commitment.

After some strategic discussion and ideas, our long-time associate professional, Scott Westman, came up with something big. Our fourth hole finishes close to the clubhouse, which inspired a new concept: the Sunset Express. We offer a bucket of balls and four holes of golf at a reasonable rate. Since we added the Sunset Express offering, it has created new green fee revenues in a timeslot where we previously registered none. There's additional significant revenue with golfers spending money in the pro shop and purchasing food and beverages too. This is just one example of the innovation of the services we offer at The Ranch.

As you reflect on your own business, there are a few important questions to consider as you look for opportunities for revenue innovation. When you look at tee sheets, do you notice common days of the week or times of the day when it's empty or half-full? There are only so many tee times per day that are available and every empty tee time is a lost opportunity for revenue. Find out why it's happening and figure out what you can do to change it. This is a great opportunity to look at the innovation within your pricing strategy. Would adding additional value beyond playing golf help fill the tee sheet? Maybe it's time to consider adding a food and beverage credit or providing a sleeve of golf balls with paid green fees in those times that are typically not busy.

Another great opportunity for revenue innovation for any business is through a loyalty program that truly works. I believe that discounting green fees isn't a good practice for your brand. However, I also believe that having a great loyalty program that rewards repeat customers is a great revenue innovation and marketing tool. A loyalty program improves your brand and keeps customers coming back time and again for the added value that they receive.

When creating a loyalty program, keep in mind that it needs to be easily accessible and usable for your guests. Punch cards are easy to lose or leave at home; people don't want another card to carry in their wallet. Your customers want to see how they are doing and how close they are to earning their next reward. It should be fun and somewhat interactive to keep your customers engaged. In today's world, with everyone carrying around smartphones, one of the best ways to engage your customers is through an app-based loyalty program. Shoppers Drug Mart, Starbucks, and 7-Eleven are three great examples of businesses that have positive, engaging, and easy-to-use loyalty program apps. Perhaps it's something to investigate for your business.

In 2017, I decided that I wanted a loyalty app for The Ranch. I literally searched the world looking for a company that had what I was looking for with no luck. After partnering with a top app builder, I created my own app from scratch—no Point of Sale (POS) system integration required. So far, it's worked exactly as I hoped and envisioned it would. Our customers love it and the app has helped our business grow in many ways. It generates new customers for us and keeps regular customers playing at The Ranch more often. For every dollar a customer spends at The Ranch, they earn points that they can redeem for free rewards like a round of golf, pro shop merchandise, gift certificates for our restaurant, and more.

After six seasons of using and creating the loyalty app, we have over 10,000 users. These users have spent just under $8 million at The Ranch. I don't believe that offering a punch card would have generated the same type of loyalty or success!

The second place where you can implement innovation at your company is in your business model. Seeking innovation in your business process can have a significant impact on your bottom line. A great example of this is innovating the way you take bookings. With COVID-19, golf has gained more popularity in the last few years. Many golf courses still don't have the infrastructure to take bookings and payments online, but if your business does, you'll stand out. One of the biggest benefits of online bookings is that you can completely sell out your tee sheet with fully prepaid guests in a matter of minutes. Previously, it would take hours of phone conversations—with higher labor costs—to book guests effectively. Although there is an initial cost up front to set up the infrastructure, the return on investment for online bookings far outweighs the setup process.

There are many positive outcomes to being innovative in your revenue innovation and your business model. Innovation is the key to long-term growth and profitability. It's important to maximize the revenue you can create with different, creative ways to generate cash flow. You need to stay ahead of your competition and innovation can help you do that. It's also important to be an industry leader as opposed to an industry follower. This helps establish and reinforce your brand. Being innovative also leaves a positive impact on your company culture; it can help the growth of your team.

Innovation can play a significant role in

shaping your company culture. It encourages your employees to think outside the box, take risks, and develop solutions to problems. When your company prioritizes innovation, it often creates a culture that values creativity, collaboration, and continuous learning, which can have a positive impact on overall employee engagement and motivation.

Innovative companies often provide employees with opportunities to experiment with new ideas and take ownership of their work. This creates a sense of autonomy, which can lead to an increase in motivation, a stronger sense of purpose, and an improvement in overall job satisfaction.

A culture of innovation can also attract and retain top talent, as employees are often drawn to organizations that encourage creativity and provide opportunities for growth and development. In this way, innovation can be a key driver of your company's success and its ability to adapt to changing market conditions, while also shaping its culture and creating a more engaged and motivated workforce.

Creating a Friendly, Inclusive Course Atmosphere

Golf has changed and evolved over the years, even more noticeably since the 2020 COVID-19 pandemic. There was a time when golf courses wanted to make their course very difficult—super fast greens, deep rough, long carries off the tees, narrow fairways, and so on. Today, that's no longer the case. Making your course easier to play and being inclusive, welcoming, and more user-friendly to golfers of all abilities is the way that golf courses should trend moving forward.

Regardless of ability, golfers want to have fun and enjoy themselves while they spend time on the course. Think about this:

- *Is it fun to spend time looking for lost golf balls?*
- *Is it fun to wait more than 20 minutes for the group in front of you to complete the hole?*
- *Is it fun to have the course marshal push you to play each hole at a quicker pace?*
- *Is it fun to feel like you're the only beginner playing the course?*

The easy answer to all of these questions is a resounding "No." It's important to have water hazards and sand traps on your course because they define its character and add to the quality and appearance. Golf needs to have challenges, but the game is hard enough on its own. Don't toughen up the course unnecessarily.

Pace of play is more important than ever with everyone having busy lives. With that, you need to keep the course moving. Cut back the rough to widen fairways and keep the rough shorter. Keep the green speed at a reasonable pace so golfers are taking three putts or less to get the ball in the cup. Playing a course with a higher bunker count will generally slow the pace of play and overall enjoyment for golfers. It's helpful to consider eliminating some of the bunkers on your course, especially if they don't serve a purpose or only impact a higher handicap player. Plus, they cost a ton of money to maintain.

Over the past several years at The Ranch, we've implemented these changes in our philosophy. It started with lowering the heights of the rough and cutting the rough and fescue further back. Both changes were extremely well-received by our guests. Then we decided to do a major bunker renovation project. We eliminated almost half of the bunkers on the course. We made some of the remaining bunkers smaller and added a few new bunkers in locations that would almost exclusively impact better players only. These changes also had a huge positive impact for The Ranch and our guests.

We added a new set of tees, called the "Express Tees," which are further up the fairway so the course can play much shorter and eliminate most of the trouble that golfers find off the tee. This strategic move helped expand our reach and attract different golfers that normally would not choose The Ranch: families, seniors, and new golfers. We also built a few new tee boxes on some holes to make a shorter carry to the fairway and cut the fairways substantially closer to the tees on other holes to help golfers succeed in finding the fairway off the tee.

All of these changes have significantly improved the overall enjoyment our guests have when playing at The Ranch. It's also cut our average pace of play down from an average of 4 hours and 25 minutes to 4 hours and 10 minutes. The course is still challenging for the lower handicap player but also fun and enjoyable for all other players. The changes have also cut back our grounds maintenance expenses. With far less square footage of sand traps to maintain, we have fewer staffing requirements, which is a win-win all the way around.

In addition to having fun on the golf course, most golfers enjoy playing in a welcoming, friendly atmosphere. How do you roll out the golf welcome mat, so to speak? And more importantly, *who* is in charge of setting the tone for the experience on your golf course? The short answer is the golf course marshal.

Every course has course marshals and every

course does its best to make golfers feel welcome while they are playing. But we can be better. And we *need* to be better. Golf marshals have been stereotyped as, "the bad guy," which tends to make players uptight and perhaps nervous when they come around. Truthfully, I don't even like the term, "marshal." The name alone seems too authoritative and unwelcoming—the opposite of what you want on your course.

We've spent some time analyzing the real role of this position at The Ranch and have rebranded it completely. We call this position a course ambassador instead of a marshal. These individuals are encouraged to engage with all groups on the course fairly early in the round to introduce themselves and let players know that they are available to help and create a fun experience at The Ranch. This helps establish an early relationship. If an ambassador needs to work with a group on their pace of play, they are instructed to clearly explain in a friendly manner that slowing the proper pace of play is impacting the enjoyment of all groups behind them.

At The Ranch, we want our ambassadors to help elevate the guests' experience in other ways. Other jobs of our ambassadors include cleaning the washrooms on the course regularly to ensure they are sparkling and held to a high standard of cleanliness. They carry a rake with them and check all bunkers on the course to rake them as needed during their shift. They also have golf balls on hand while they circulate the course; if they discover a group searching for a lost ball, they will offer a few from their stash to replace it. This keeps the group moving forward, and the gesture is usually appreciated.

The ambassadors have a few other tools in their toolbox to help in special situations. For example, should an ambassador see a golfer hit an incredible shot, he could offer the golfer a sleeve of balls or a pint of beer as a reward. If an ambassador is working with a group on their pace of play and they catch up and help other players on the course play at the proper place, the ambassador could offer the players a jug of draft beer or a plate of nachos to thank them for their efforts. Our ambassadors also carry around lollipops to offer guests and on days that are very hot they will offer popsicles. The course marshal doesn't have to be the bad guy. If you think outside the box, they could play a key role in the golfer experience and help take the service at your club to a higher level.

Before we move on, there's one point we need to discuss: the role of women in golf since the sport has historically been male-dominated. Just as men do, women love to play golf, enjoy buying items in your pro shop, and look forward to visiting the 19th hole for food and cocktails after a round.

As you may or may not know, the number of ladies playing golf is growing rapidly. It's important to understand what makes for an enjoyable experience in their eyes. If you're not paying attention to their wants and needs, they may take their money elsewhere. Have you taken the time to ask women coming to your club what they do or don't like about playing your course? Are you giving women the best chance to enjoy their experience at your course? Is your course ready to support women in their game?

Honestly, and sadly, I never considered the golf experience from a woman's perspective until I met my wife and her family. This led me to playing plenty of golf with my wife and my mother-in-law. It also led to many conversations with them and their friends about their experiences on the golf course.

My eyes were opened when I realized that The Ranch was missing the boat. We needed to become more women-friendly. Do you have holes on your course where the forward tees are further back than the blue and white tees to make it a Par 5 for those playing the forward tees rather than a Par 4? I'd bet a lot of money that if you surveyed those who play the forward tees at your course, there would be a high percentage that don't enjoy it. I would bet the majority would prefer to play it as a Par 4 and would find the course more enjoyable if a tee box was built further up on the fairway. It's generally not well-received by golfers to play a course with different pars.

There are other details to consider, too. Think about the merchandise that you offer for women. Is shopping in the pro shop a positive experience? Do you offer trendy and stylish clothing options for women? Make sure you have a good product mix and proper space in your pro shop to proudly display women's merchandise. Do you have food and drink menu items that appeal to all guests? Having menu selections that include healthier, lighter options are appealing and will encourage all types of guests to stay after a round to relax and unwind.

Make sure your course is welcoming and friendly, and ensure that everyone who plays has a great experience. The importance of an inclusive golf atmosphere can't be overstated!

Empowering Your Employees

I'm going to let you in on a little secret: you cannot and will not run a successful business on your own. To be successful, you need to surround yourself with great people who are extremely capable in the roles they've been given. It's important to engage and empower your team to execute their roles effectively. But it's just as important to use your staff's ideas. Give your staff a voice by regularly soliciting and acting on their feedback. Your team is in the trenches working hard every day. They have their fingers on the pulse of your operation and they will have some excellent thoughts and ideas to help take your business to the next level.

Empowering your team can create exponential benefits for your organization. It starts with the creation of trust in the leadership of your business. This trust, along with enabling teammates to actively contribute, will see your staff motivation reach new heights. Your team will think more creatively as they realize their thoughts and ideas will be heard and respected. Together, these attributes will lead to an increase in your bottom line.

To empower your employees, you need to listen to them and recognize them. For example, have regular brainstorming sessions where your team is encouraged to share thoughts and ideas. Regular staff meetings are another opportunity to listen and communicate with your team. One-on-one communication is also extremely important. It helps you get to know your team on a more personal level and some employees may feel more comfortable sharing ideas this way rather than in a group setting. Recognition of your staff is another key part of motivating and getting the best effort out of your team. If you use and implement ideas from an employee, be sure to give them credit and acknowledgment for their input. It will help them understand their value and realize that their contributions are greatly appreciated. It will also keep motivation high and retention levels strong.

At The Ranch, our golf course superintendent suggested to me that we offer opportunities where we allow our customers to bring dogs with them to the course when they play. I was very surprised that he would want dogs on the course, but I was open to the idea, as he thought it would bring attention to us and get people talking about us. I sat on the idea for a bit and when I had a meeting with a nearby business, Champion Pet Foods, about working as partners, I pitched the idea of working together on a golf with dogs event. They jumped on board and it was a huge success. Golfers loved bringing their dogs to the course with them and we got an incredible amount of local media exposure and even some national media exposure. An incredible success that was all stimulated from a conversation with our superintendent who was happy to contribute his thoughts on trying something outside the box.

Empowered employees are more likely to be engaged and motivated to do their work well, which will lead to increased productivity and better results. When employees are given the authority to make decisions, they are more likely to make informed choices that benefit the company. Empowered employees are more likely to take ownership of their work and go the extra mile to ensure customer satisfaction. When employees feel trusted and valued, they are more likely to be satisfied with their jobs and stay with the company long-term. Empowered employees are more likely to think outside the box and come up with innovative solutions to problems. Overall, empowering your employees can lead to a more positive work culture, increased employee engagement and retention, and better business outcomes.

Taking a Swing at Corporate Sales

Is your club or business doing as well as it can in corporate sales? How can you take your corporate sales to new heights?

One way to increase your corporate sales is by selling branded or corporate merchandise to other companies. This is a strategy that golf courses have used for years. It's a nice way to increase your revenue and profit, plus it keeps your staff busy during the off-season, which is a bonus. The key takeaway to selling branded merchandise is to start by targeting the companies that you already have relationships with. If your club has members, perhaps the businesses that they work for have a need for logo products, such as hats, shirts, drinkware, etc., that you offer.

Another option is to approach the organizers of the golf tournaments that your club hosts to see if they need first tee gifts or other branded products to give away or auction off as part of the tournament. This choice is fairly easy because you likely have a close relationship with the individuals who run the golf tournaments. Everyone has relationships and friendships that they can contact to drum up more business for the branded products you offer. This approach alone could potentially add a nice amount of revenue and profit to your bottom line.

One final way to help grow your corporate sales is by using social media to bring awareness to your offerings. You can create great content that will draw attention and engagement to your posts so that they don't get lost while a user is scrolling. Quick videos and photos can help with this strategy.

As you grow your reach and take your sales to the next level, there are two factors that you need to be aware of that work against golf courses in this space:

- The common perception that golf courses are expensive places to shop.
- The common perception that golf courses can only supply golf merchandise instead of promotional products and that it's easier to use a traditional promotional products company for branded products.

Neither of these perceptions is accurate, but these are prevalent beliefs among product buyers. To truly be successful in the corporate sales space at your golf course or business, you'll need to find a way to change the perceptions of your potential customers.

At The Ranch, we solved the perception issue by branding our own promotional products company. Tough Stuff Promotions was born to truly get into the market by eliminating the impression that our prices would be too high. As a legitimate promotional products company, Tough Stuff helped us establish relationships with the same suppliers that all promotional companies buy from. This expanded our offerings to almost anything and everything you could ever dream of putting a logo on.

The two misconceptions I described earlier were answered with this move, and our sales skyrocketed quickly. We even became the sole supplier of branded products to a nationwide company. We didn't have the overhead of building an administration staff that our competitors did, because we operate Tough Stuff out of the golf course. When it makes sense, we rely on and share the fact that Tough Stuff is indeed owned by The Ranch. This detail enables us to wine and dine our potential customers with golf and host them in our restaurant at a low cost, unlike our competitors. You may not necessarily need to go as far as we did to eliminate the misconceptions with your potential customers. However, Tough Stuff Promotions is a great example of innovative thinking that has helped to grow our business at The Ranch.

The Pandemic Impact on Business

In 2020, the COVID-19 pandemic changed our lives forever. In some ways, these changes are likely permanent. Unfortunately, golf is not excluded from this. Golf in Canada boomed during the pandemic, and The Ranch was fortunate enough to be packed every day. However, the cadence of golf and its routines were dramatically altered. And The Ranch was one of the few courses that the pandemic negatively impacted in a big way.

Tournaments and other events were not allowed to happen at The Ranch—period. As the busiest tournament golf course in the province, losing the ability to host all of our events majorly cost us in revenue. We were still busy, but our business model changed and we had to adapt. We weren't able to employ nearly the same number of people since we weren't hosting banquets and events. Our pro shop sales were dropping without tournament prizes. We were forced to have greeters in the parking lots. Tee times had to be spaced further apart. Only one person was allowed to ride in a power cart. Green fees were strongly recommended to be paid online or over the phone. Ball washers were not allowed on the course nor were rakes allowed in sand traps. It was a lot of change for all the golf course operators to manage.

During the pandemic, we learned quickly and made adjustments on the fly. These are findings that we will take forward to ensure our business operates even better in the future. Over time, restrictions relaxed and some things did return to the former way of operating.

Now that the pandemic is over and much of our lives have returned to a "new" normal, I can say from experience that golf courses and their staff grew so much after functioning during a pandemic. Many of these "pandemic" procedures may stay forever. For example, operations budgets will stay leaner with so many unknowns.

Some of these changes will help golf courses move forward if they maintain the learnings that came from dealing with COVID-19 for the last few years. Here are a few examples of how golf course departments can take advantage of their learnings in a post-pandemic setting. At The Ranch, we follow these protocols:

Grounds

- Finding efficiencies in mowing and other lawn care/landscaping to operate with minimal staff
- Using the help of all-year-round staff for laying tarps in the fall and removing tarps in the spring
- Cleaning the on-course restrooms more frequently

Food & Beverage

- QR codes to access menus on smartphones rather than printed menus
- Stringent cleaning and sanitation duties

- Hand sanitizer available throughout the clubhouse
- Creative options for food service on the course
- Increased hours and service of the beverage cart and/or snack shack
- Streamlined, limited offering menus

Pro Shop

- More online bookings
- Prepaid green fees online
- Cautious buying plans to limit the risk of excess inventory and leave room for in-season purchases
- Condensed number of vendors carried in the shop

The change that has had the most profound impact on our business is the prepaid green free. When you buy tickets to a concert or sporting event, you always pay for tickets in advance. Refunds aren't given if you change your mind about going, and it's your responsibility to sell or give away your tickets. Similarly, on a golf course, prepaid fees eliminate the no-show problem and make the day-of-play experience smoother. Sure, if the individual booking doesn't want to pay for the group's green fees, arrangements must be made to pay back the person who books the tee time. With e-transfer and PayPal, it's easy.

When there are only seven or eight tee times available per hour, each tee time at a golf course is extremely valuable to both the course and the golfers who want to play. Groups that no-show or show up with fewer players than they book for are a huge problem at public golf courses. No-shows cost clubs tons of revenue and prevent others from booking tee times that could have been played.

The concept of prepaid green fees doesn't make all customers happy, but the positive outcomes for The Ranch make it highly unlikely that we will ever go back to the way green fees were handled pre-pandemic. As a public golf course, we generally had 12 to 24 players no-show on their daily tee times. Whether it's an entire foursome not showing up or groups booked for four players that only have two or three players show up, the lost revenue adds up over the course of a golf season. During Covid we followed the recommended protocol of prepaid green fees to do what we felt was best to protect our customers and staff. We found that no-shows were significantly less frequent and we were no longer losing revenue.

If proper notice is given, golf courses absolutely should be reasonable with their refunds and rain check policies. If proper notice is not given, just like other events, the golf course should not need to compensate you, especially if last-minute notice was given and there was no ability to resell the tee time.

We also followed the protocol to have our tee times spread out further apart. From this change, we saw a faster pace of play and improved overall enjoyment for our guests, which were two huge benefits. When the restrictions dropped, we decided to keep doing what we were doing. We kept the prepaid green fees and we kept tee time intervals 10 minutes apart instead of the eight or nine-minute split from before the pandemic. We invested the money we gained from not having no-shows back into the overall guest experience at The Ranch by keeping tee times spread further apart. This decision has been a win-win for The Ranch and all of our guests.

Before the pandemic, very few courses were

set up to handle prepaid green fees. Although this is changing now with technology, the majority of courses are unlikely to make the switch. However, I feel that prepaid green fees will stick around at some courses. As more golf courses recognize and understand the benefits of prepaid green fees, there's no question that more clubs will adopt this policy as standard procedure.

As the restrictions finally ended and some sense of normalcy returned, our business quickly reverted back to the way it was pre-pandemic. Tournaments came back in full force. In 2022, we hosted the most tournament rounds in the history of the golf course. In 2023, those numbers will climb even higher. The pandemic was tough on all of us in many different ways, but we learned from it and we put our learnings to good use to continue improving our business.

Giving Back to the Industry

The idea of having my own radio show on TSN 1260 was never something I thought of on my own. In fact, several years ago, TSN 1260 approached me with the idea of hosting a golf show on their station. I went into the meeting thinking that they would want me to be an employee of the radio station and that the offer would be for me to plan some content each week, show up to the station, and talk golf on air. This was nothing close to the offer. TSN 1260 wanted the show to be my own business where I would pay them for the airtime, sell all the advertising on my own, and then keep the ad revenue. At the time in my life, this seemed like a ton of work, and I declined the opportunity.

A couple of years later in 2019, TSN 1260 approached me again. This time, I knew what to expect and did my homework. My personal situation was quite different as well. My wife, Jessica, was pregnant and was going to be on maternity leave. With the new addition to our family approaching, I thought the timing was perfect. The radio show was an opportunity for me to bring in some extra revenue for our growing household. I reached out to my friend, Jason Gregor, who had his own show on the station for years which had a similar setup. He was a thorough source of information leading up to my meeting. The discussion went as I had expected and I asked for permission to tell people about this opportunity to see if I could get some interest from potential advertisers. The feedback I received was positive, so I signed an agreement with TSN 1260 and the radio show was a reality. In its first season, it was called the YEG Golf Show. Now, it's the VIP Golf Show, thanks to the title sponsor of the same name.

I had some reservations about doing the show on my own, as it was something new for me. I thought having someone else to talk with on the show was the way to go. My friend Curtis Stock was the long-time golf writer for the *Edmonton Journal* and *Edmonton Sun* and a semi-regular invite to the Sunday matches. He was very well-known and respected in the golf community and I thought he would be an excellent co-host. I shared with him what was happening and asked if he wanted to do the show with me. He agreed to be the show's co-host and the on-air duo was official.

I had done a ton of TV and radio interviews in my life through golf and hockey, but hosting a radio show was totally different. I was responsible for carrying the show and creating its content. There wasn't much training involved prior to the startup of the show. One day, Curtis and I met at the radio station, put on our headsets, and did a mock segment of us just chatting golf for 15 minutes. We didn't really have anything prepared for that test run and 15 minutes felt like an eternity. It was a great exercise that taught me that I was going to need to be very prepared each week.

The radio show runs an hour and a half each Sunday, from 8:30 a.m. to 10 a.m. for 20 weeks out of the year. I don't have an exact routine for prep work prior to the show, but I do a ton of research and planning in the spring. I brainstorm show topics and guests, find advertisers, and line up the content. During the year, I generally spend one or two hours each week doing the final prep work and confirming guests.

We have now completed four years of the show and I recently signed an agreement for two more years. The show has been successful, even winning the Edmonton Readers Choice Award one year as Edmonton's Favorite Talk Radio Show. We have become more comfortable on-air as time went on, and I have come to genuinely love going to the station on Sunday mornings to do the show. I find it a bit sad each year when the show ends for the season. It truly is an honor to do the show and promote the game of golf in this way. It's always a lot of fun piecing together the lineup of guests for the show, trying to think of topics and guests that will ensure that the listeners have the opportunity to be entertained and learn things about the different aspects of the game.

It has been a great journey so far, and I look forward to continuing with the radio show for many years to come. I enjoy it so much that I would consider finding ways to go deeper into golf media should opportunities be presented that make sense. This was a terrific opportunity that I am fortunate to have come my way and am so thrilled that it has worked out as it has.

After becoming a head professional, I knew it would be important to get more involved with the PGA of Alberta and give back to the golf community and the association. In business, giving your time and knowledge is such an important thing. You can learn and grow from your experiences, and it strengthens your community. Giving back also allows you to use your public speaking, organization, communication, and other skills outside of your workplace.

In 1994, things at the PGA of Alberta looked a little different than it does today. I was at the Nanton Golf Club and the association was basically a one-man operation that Dave Mayes ran out of his house–then a small office–at the Heritage Pointe Golf Club south of Calgary. He needed a volunteer to take over the Southern Alberta Head Professional Series, which was a series of golf tournaments that head professionals in Southern Alberta would participate in. I jumped at the opportunity because I thought it would be a great way to help the association. Plus it was a good networking opportunity to meet and grow relationships with the head professionals in Southern Alberta.

To get started, I contacted all the golf courses and found facilities that were interested and available to host events. After solidifying the schedule, I connected with all the head professionals about the schedule and communicated how they could enter. I also created a bank account specifically for the HP Series. The PGA had a sponsor for the series and they would send me a check for the bank account, which I would divide up among all the events. For every event, I handled all the money. As an event drew closer, I did the draw and communicated tee times to all the players. I also played in the events by making sure I gave myself the first tee time so that I could be in the first group to manage the scoring. After my round, once the event was completed, I congratulated the winner and headed back to Nanton where I determined the breakdown of the cash payouts to the top performers. Lastly, I'd write checks and mail them out. It was a ton of work, but I was happy to do it and I enjoyed the opportunity to meet many new people. I volunteered for this position for two seasons. By then, the PGA of Alberta grew large enough to handle the tournaments through the main office.

From 2012 to 2018, I was on the Board of Directors for the PGA of Alberta. It was another great opportunity to give back and work with some of the best, brightest, and most passionate minds in the business and help shape the future of the association. The PGA of Alberta has had tremendous staff members over the years who have done great work on behalf of its members. For most of my time on the board, I was the chair of the Promotion and Communication committees. With the Communication Committee, the biggest hurdle was navigating social media, as it was brand-new at the time. We wanted to tread lightly and see where it would go. One other board member and I were the only two people who had access to the association's Twitter account in the beginning. Times have definitely changed, as social media is such a key component of communications now.

The Promotion Committee's main focus was the PGA of Alberta Consumer Shows that happen annually in Calgary and Edmonton. These shows are a big production and are one of the key revenue sources for the association. It was a pleasure to work with the PGA staff on these events for several years. The events were a great way for golf courses to showcase their mission to consumers and a welcome networking opportunity for industry peers after a long winter. Although the shows were on pause during the COVID-19 pandemic, they are set to return in 2023. As with many other things, I stepped down from the board when my term ended, just before my son was born. But it was a rewarding experience to give back and get involved with the association as a board member. I'd definitely consider volunteering with the board again in the future.

Before and after my time on the board, I always stayed involved with the PGA by being a part of various committees that support the board and the staff in many aspects. Currently, I'm on the Award and Consumer Show committees.

Another way that I give back to the PGA is to accept offers to be a presenter or be on a panel at various events and educational seminars. It's always an honor to be asked to contribute to an educational forum or event because I'm happy to share my knowledge and experience with others in the industry and drum up excitement for individuals who may be new to the golf world. I am also involved with the PGA of Alberta Mentorship program where I am available and accessible to new professionals in the industry to help guide them in their own journey.

I feel fortunate that Phil Berube became the executive director of the Alberta Golf Association. Amateur Golf is also very important and when he started in this role he was able to engage with me and show me the value in his organization. I am thrilled to work closely with him and his team in hosting competitive amateur events and assist with Alberta Golf in any way that Phil requires.

No matter what business you're in, find a way to give back. It could be small, like volunteering to help at an event, or it could be larger, like running a committee or hosting a silent auction to raise funds. Giving back supports your community in so many different ways, and your help is priceless.

I hope that my story and business journey inspire you to do great things. Remember, you are in charge of your success. You're ready to take on any challenge that comes your way, and you can do anything that you set your mind to doing.

I hope that the business principles in this book, especially knowing who you are as a brand and finding ways to stand out from your competition, guide your path to success. Whether you open a new restaurant, start a brewery, or build a real estate empire from the ground up, you have the keys to success right here in this book. Refer back to them as often as you need.

Lastly, don't forget to support and give back to your community. Find ways to volunteer your time and your talents. Your community will thank you and remember your actions.

Afterword

Thank you so much for taking the time to read *Outside the Tee Box*. I hope you enjoyed learning about my journey in life, business, and some of the concepts that I strongly believe in that lead to success in business.

The thought of writing a book had never crossed my mind until I met mentor, friend, and fellow Chicago Blackhawk fan, Kraig Kann. Kraig has written his own book after a lengthy career as a host on the Golf Channel and with the LPGA Tour. He was a keynote speaker at a virtual seminar put on by the PGA of Alberta. I loved everything about his presentation and reached out to him after the seminar. I continued working with Kraig on some business and

Afterword

personal branding and developed a great relationship with him. In our work together, Kraig suggested that I write a book of my own. This idea sounded scary to me in the beginning—I'm not the most outgoing person. Putting myself out there in this way seemed daunting. He challenged me to get out of my comfort zone, and here we are.

A couple of key points that I hope you took away from reading the book are first: to figure out exactly who you are as a business or as an individual and truly *be* what you are. No one person can be great at everything, just as it isn't realistic to think a business can satisfy the variety of needs that different people require. By discovering this and staying focused on being the best version of yourself in this space, it will absolutely lead to success.

Secondly, the need to elevate what you do or what your business does to separate yourself from your competition is so important to your future success. If you or your business do what everyone else does, then you won't be the person others seek for a step up in your career. Potential customers won't view your business as a place they feel they need to support. Find ways to

Afterword

differentiate what you are doing that will make people take notice of what you are doing. Success will soon follow.

What is next for me and The Ranch? My desire to continue to learn and grow will never stop. I will continue to seek ways to improve what we do at The Ranch each and every year to keep us as busy and successful as we are. I am fortunate to have built a tremendous management team that are passionate and dedicated to their work at The Ranch. They all plan to be here long-term and with that, together, we will do everything within our control to ensure our guests have the best experience that we can provide. The three pillars of our success—premier conditions, top-notch service, and unmatched value—are what we will strive to provide day in and day out for many years to come.

As for me personally, I have found true happiness in my life. I have an amazing wife and a wonderful son that I get to enjoy sharing life with. I will carry on with my passion for health and fitness to ensure I am healthy and get to enjoy my family for a long time watching Luke grow up and see where his life goes. The Ranch

Afterword

is my pride and joy and my other family. I look forward to coming to work every day and would not want anything more in my golf career. As the radio show heads into Season 5 this spring, I have found another passion with that and am truly honored to be able to promote golf in this way. I am hopeful that I will continue working with TSN 1260 for many years hosting the show.

    I enjoyed writing this book very much. Streamline Books was a perfect choice for me to work with. Will Severns and Alex Demczak own Streamline Books and were both very encouraging and supportive throughout the process. Trevor Waite was the project manager of the book and he kept everything on track and moving in the right direction. Chris Yingling did a great job assisting with the editing of the book. Allison Lewis was the main editor of the book and who I worked with the most. She is amazing at what she does and it was a true honor to work closely with her. Thank you to everyone who took the time to read this book. I hope you enjoyed it and found it helpful in some way.

About the Author

Murray McCourt grew up in Stettler, Alberta, a small town in the province of Alberta, Canada. He always had passions in his life, whether it was his favorite professional sports teams, being the GM of a Junior Hockey team, or his health and fitness journey. Of all his passions, besides his wife Jessica and son Luke, his biggest passion is the game of golf and the golf business. This passion has led to a very successful career over the past 30+ years. Murray has been the General Manager/Executive Professional and part owner of The Ranch Golf and Country Club since

2007. He has won the PGA of Alberta Top 100 Award, Club Professional of the Year, & Executive Professional of the Year. The Ranch Golf & Country Club has appeared in *Score Golf Magazine* Top 100 courses in Canada and in 2021 *Score* ranked The Ranch as the second-best course in Alberta by value and 30th in Canada.

If you would like more information about The Ranch, you can visit our website at www.theranchgolf.com. You can also check out The Ranch on Twitter (@ranchgolfcourse), Instagram (@ranchgolfcourse), Tik Tok (@ranchgolfcourse) or Facebook. If you wish to connect with me personally, I can be reached via email at gm@theranchgolf.com. Best of luck on your future endeavors!

Manufactured by Amazon.ca
Bolton, ON

33086107R00111